Excitin

Dear Readers,

We are excited to announce major updates in this new edition of the book (fifth edition):

- A new chapter discussing the importance of customer relationship management (CRM) to the overall financial success of the organization has been added. This chapter also explores the topic of customer profitability analysis and its significance for the organization.

- The content of each chapter has been fully updated and reflects the current trends in cost accounting and management.

- Additional problem-based exercises have been included on the basis of real-world problems that many professionals face in the workforce. This 5th edition also contains many case studies that highlight real-world problems and current affairs.

- This 5th edition has more content coverage, which will appeal to modern students interested in reading relevant information about the world of cost accounting and management.

- This updated edition includes detailed and self-explanatory solutions to unsolved examples in Practice Exercises. You may download the solutions at www.vibrantpublishers/onlineresources

THIS BOOK IS AVAILABLE IN E-BOOK, PAPERBACK(B/W) AND HARDBACK(COLOR) FORMAT.

SELF-LEARNING MANAGEMENT SERIES

TITLE	PAPERBACK* ISBN
ACCOUNTING, FINANCE & ECONOMICS	
COST ACCOUNTING AND MANAGEMENT ESSENTIALS	9781636511030
FINANCIAL ACCOUNTING ESSENTIALS	9781636510972
FINANCIAL MANAGEMENT ESSENTIALS	9781636511009
MACROECONOMICS ESSENTIALS	9781636511818
MICROECONOMICS ESSENTIALS	9781636511153
PERSONAL FINANCE ESSENTIALS	9781636511849
ENTREPRENEURSHIP & STRATEGY	
BUSINESS PLAN ESSENTIALS	9781636511214
BUSINESS STRATEGY ESSENTIALS	9781949395778
ENTREPRENEURSHIP ESSENTIALS	9781636511603
GENERAL MANAGEMENT	
BUSINESS LAW ESSENTIALS	9781636511702
DECISION MAKING ESSENTIALS	9781636510026
LEADERSHIP ESSENTIALS	9781636510316
PRINCIPLES OF MANAGEMENT ESSENTIALS	9781636511542
TIME MANAGEMENT ESSENTIALS	9781636511665

*Also available in Hardback & Ebook formats

SELF-LEARNING MANAGEMENT SERIES

TITLE	PAPERBACK* ISBN

HUMAN RESOURCE MANAGEMENT

Title	ISBN
DIVERSITY IN THE WORKPLACE ESSENTIALS	9781636511122
HR ANALYTICS ESSENTIALS	9781636510347
HUMAN RESOURCE MANAGEMENT ESSENTIALS	9781949395839
ORGANIZATIONAL BEHAVIOR ESSENTIALS	9781636510378
ORGANIZATIONAL DEVELOPMENT ESSENTIALS	9781636511481

MARKETING & SALES MANAGEMENT

Title	ISBN
DIGITAL MARKETING ESSENTIALS	9781949395747
MARKETING MANAGEMENT ESSENTIALS	9781636511788
SALES MANAGEMENT ESSENTIALS	9781636510743
SERVICES MARKETING ESSENTIALS	9781636511733

OPERATIONS & PROJECT MANAGEMENT

Title	ISBN
AGILE ESSENTIALS	9781636510057
OPERATIONS & SUPPLY CHAIN MANAGEMENT ESSENTIALS	9781949395242
PROJECT MANAGEMENT ESSENTIALS	9781636510712
STAKEHOLDER ENGAGEMENT ESSENTIALS	9781636511511

*Also available in Hardback & Ebook formats

This page is intentionally left blank

SELF-LEARNING MANAGEMENT SERIES

COST ACCOUNTING AND MANAGEMENT ESSENTIALS

YOU ALWAYS WANTED TO KNOW

FIFTH EDITION

A simple guide to making managerial decisions based on cost data

KALPESH ASHAR

Cost Accounting and Management Essentials You Always Wanted To Know
Fifth Edition

Paperback ISBN 10: 1-63651-103-1
Paperback ISBN 13: 978-1-63651-103-0

Ebook ISBN 10: 1-63651-104-X
Ebook ISBN 13: 978-1-63651-104-7

Hardback ISBN 10: 1-63651-105-8
Hardback ISBN 13: 978-1-63651-105-4

Library of Congress Control Number: 2011928208

This publication is designed to provide accurate and authoritative information in regard to the subject matter covered. The Author has made every effort in the preparation of this book to ensure the accuracy of the information. However, information in this book is sold without warranty either expressed or implied. The Author or the Publisher will not be liable for any damages caused or alleged to be caused either directly or indirectly by this book.

Vibrant Publishers books are available at special quantity discount for sales promotions, or for use in corporate training programs. For more information please write to bulkorders@vibrantpublishers.com

Please email feedback / corrections (technical, grammatical or spelling) to spellerrors@vibrantpublishers.com

To access the complete catalogue of Vibrant Publishers, visit www.vibrantpublishers.com

About the Author

Kalpesh Ashar is a management consultant and corporate trainer holding an MBA (Dean's Award Winner) from SPJIMR, one of Asia's top business schools, and an Engineering degree with honors in Electronics. He has over 24 years of experience in large organizations and start-ups in Asia, USA, and Europe.

Kalpesh has worked in several project management roles, like Senior Project Manager, Delivery Manager, and Program Manager. He is passionate about writing on management subjects. His techno-business background gives him a unique position to write on management topics that are easy to understand for non-MBA graduates. His books are authored in a simple to understand manner without unnecessary use of management jargon.

Other contributors

Virginia Eron Frondozo is a Certified Public Accountant and holds a Bachelor of Science degree in Business Administration. She was. the head of Cost Accounting in Colgate-Palmolive Philippines, Inc. and was instrumental in developing her team to assume expanded roles in the organization to include managerial finance functions. In mid-2013, Virginia left the corporate world and started accepting online consultancy engagements ranging from business analysis and business planning to coaching and tutoring.

Mark Koscinski, a certified public accountant, is an assistant professor of accounting practice at Moravian University in Bethlehem, Pennsylvania where he teaches a wide range of accounting courses and decision analysis. Dr. Koscinski is the author of *Decision Making Essentials You Always Wanted to Know*, another book in the Self-Learning Management Series. He has over 40 years of experience in accounting and management in the banking, pharmaceutical, defence contracting and toy industries. Dr. Koscinski has degrees in economics, accounting, taxation, and personal financial planning. He also maintains an active consulting practice.

What experts say about this book!

The book uses charts, graphics, tables and relevant examples to explain the concepts of cost accounting and also provides a detailed computation for each of them. Cost Accounting and Management Essentials is a well-organized book that will help students understand and conquer the subject easily.

**– Jangho Gil, Assistant Professor of Accounting,
Monmouth University Logo**

The book is simple to understand, contains a plethora of questions and answers and is perfect for those who are studying cost accounting as a non-core subject. This book is broken down into bite-sized pieces so that the concepts of cost accounting are easy to digest and remember.

**– Xihui Chen, Assistant Professor of Accounting and Finance,
Heriot-Watt University**

What experts say about this book!

The book touches upon all the concepts required in cost accounting without getting into a lot of details. It introduces the readers to a lot of terminologies when it comes to cost classifications and behaviors.

– Dr Cheryl A Moore, Assistant Professor of Accounting, Mercyhurst University

This book covers adequate topics that are included in the PG curriculum in recent years. The theoretical coverage and language of the book is lucid and student-friendly. The illustrations are better placed and the book has simple examples that help elucidate the concepts. Overall, the book offers a clear understanding of cost and management accounting.

– Dr.Chetana Asbe, Faculty of Finance, Chetana's Institute of Management & Research

Table of Contents

This page is intentionally left blank

Preface

Managers need to make quick and correct decisions on an almost daily basis. But to make these decisions, they need to understand various numbers about their business. These numbers are provided by a cost accounting system. In today's economic environment, this kind of decision making is not only limited to the senior management, but also done by managers and leaders at all levels in the hierarchy.

Cost Accounting and Management Essentials You Always Wanted to Know provides that set of bare minimum skills that you need to understand the costing numbers. It consists of only those key areas that are considered critical. The objective of the book is not to teach you everything in costing, but to equip you with enough information to be more productive and accurate in your decision making, with the cost perspective in mind.

This page is intentionally left blank

Who can benefit from the book?

This book can be used by anyone who needs to understand cost accounting numbers, like:

- Managers in an organization

- Individuals who need to make decisions in an organization

- Senior management of an organization

It can also be beneficial for those interested in the field of cost accounting, like:

- Students learning costing as part of their university course

- Anyone else who is interested in learning how to read costing numbers to help in decision making

How to use this book?

The recommended approach to reading this book is to start from the first chapter and go in sequence, even if you are experienced in costing. This will ensure that you get a solid base of the previous chapters that will be needed to understand the later chapters better. There is a lot of cost accounting terminology in each chapter that could be new to you, and understanding it will help you with the later material in the book.

This page is intentionally left blank

Chapter **1**

Introduction

In this chapter, we shall look at the fundamentals of cost accounting. These form the pillars for our understanding of the later chapters.

The key learning objectives of this chapter are:

- Learn the different terms used in cost / managerial accounting

- Understand the different types of costs

- Get introduced to a costing system for decision-making

An accounting system helps capture and organize information related to business transactions. Depending upon the focus, it can be divided into two types – Financial Accounting and Managerial Accounting. A Financial Accounting system contains financial statements and disclosures meant for decision makers external to the company. A Managerial Accounting system contains detailed plans and performance reports meant for decision-makers within the company.

Figure 1.1

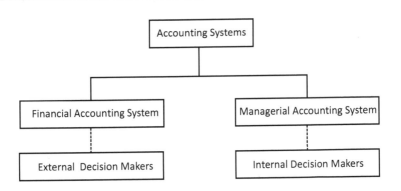

Cost Accounting provides information required by both types of accounting systems. Another term, Cost Management, is also used frequently. It refers to the approaches and activities adopted by managers to use the company's resources to increase the value given to customers and to achieve organizational goals. It must be noted that cost management is not synonymous with cost reduction.

In the later chapters, we shall look at the cost accounting and cost management aspects of accounting. We shall see how cost accounting information helps in short-term tactical and long-term strategic decision making.

1.1 Cost Accounting Terms

This section sets a foundation for the rest of the book by describing the most important terms used in cost accounting. An understanding of these terms will help in later sections to understand how costs work, how they are reported, and how decisions are taken using them.

Cost Object

Cost object is the product or service with respect to which cost needs to be computed. For example, if a car manufacturer wants to assess costs, the cars that they manufacture would be their cost object. Similarly, the cost object for a bank would be its customer accounts. Costs are classified on the basis of the cost object.

Direct and Indirect Costs

Costs are classified under two categories as given below:

Direct Costs

These are costs that can be directly traced or caused by a product, service, project, organizational unit, or activity. For example, the cost of a steering wheel is a direct cost in the manufacturing of a car. Similarly, the cost of effort undertaken by a worker in making the doors of the car also amounts to direct cost. Below are some examples of direct costs:

a) Cost of cement used in the construction of a building

b) Cost of tires used in building a car

c) Cost of a project management consultant in the construction of a bridge

Indirect Costs

These are costs that cannot be directly traced to a single product, service, project, organizational unit, or activity. These costs are allocated rather than being traced to individual products or services as there is no cost-effective way of tracing them directly. This allocation can be done in several ways, as described in detail later. For example, the rent of a plant used to manufacture cars of multiple varieties cannot be directly traced to every car model. Hence, the rent is an indirect cost. If the plant were to manufacture only one car model, then the rent would become a direct cost. Similarly, the cost of supervisors for various products of the company is also an indirect cost and needs to be allocated in some proportion instead of being directly traced to the products. Below are some examples of indirect costs:

a) Salary of staff in corporate headquarters

b) Cost of adhesive used in creating various products of the company. This is especially because it may not be cost-effective to try and relate this cost directly to each product. It would be much better to allocate this cost on a certain basis (an estimation)

c) Cost of power in a plant making many different products

Variable and Fixed Costs

When a company changes the number of products and/or services it provides, its total costs would also change. However, some costs change in relation to quantity or volume whereas others do not. On this basis, these are the following categories of costs: Variable Costs and Fixed Costs.

Variable Costs

Costs that change proportionately with volume are called variable costs. So, if the company sells 10% more products, its variable costs would also go up by 10%. For example, the cost of car tires is variable and so is the cost of the steering wheel. We saw earlier that both these costs are also Direct costs. Hence, a certain cost can be Direct and at the same time, Variable. Below are some other examples of variable costs.

a) Cost of paint required for a house

b) Cost of labor for manufacturing a truck

c) Cost of wood in constructing a house

The diagram and table below show how variable costs behave.

Figure 1.2

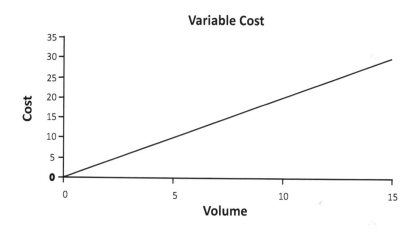

Table 1.1

Units produced	Variable cost per unit	Total variable cost
10	$500	$5,000
50	$500	$25,000
200	$500	$100,000

Non-variable/Fixed Costs

These are exactly the opposite of variable costs. They do not vary with the quantity or volume of the product manufactured or the service provided. This means that this cost is independent of the volume. For example, the rent of office premises is a fixed cost as it does not change with the change in business volume.

Below are some examples of fixed costs:

   a) Cost of assembly line for a car model

   b) Cost of supervisors

   c) Cost of rent paid by a bank branch office

However, it may be noted that fixed costs are generally fixed within a certain relevant range. For example, if the business grows so much that a new office will have to be bought to accommodate the new machinery and personnel, then the rent cost changes. Hence, it is said to be fixed only over a certain volume of business called the relevant range. The diagram and table below show how fixed costs behave over the relevant range.

Figure 1.3

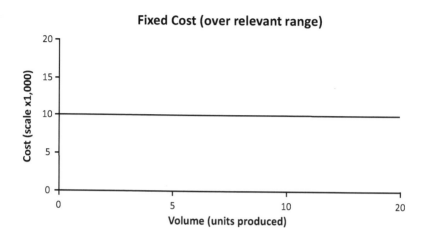

Fixed Cost (over relevant range)

Table 1.2

Total Fixed cost	Units produced	Fixed cost per unit
$10,000	5	$2,000
$10,000	10	$1,000
$10,000	20	$500

Fixed costs are generally chunky costs or a step-function, as they are incurred in chunks when one goes outside the relevant range. So, if a new office is to be bought for additional space, the fixed cost would increase by a large chunk equal to the rent of the new office. It will then stay fixed until the business grows beyond another higher relevant range. The following diagram and table show how fixed costs behave across different relevant ranges.

Figure 1.4

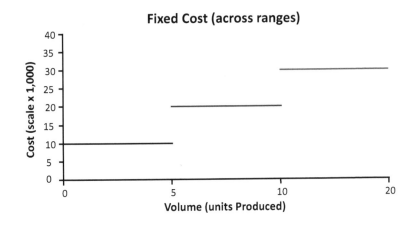

Fixed Cost (across ranges)

Table 1.3

Total Fixed cost	Units produced	Fixed cost per unit
$10,000	3	$3,333
$10,000	4	$2,500
$20,000	6	$3,333
$20,000	7	$2,857
$30,000	11	$2,727
$30,000	15	$2,000

Semi-variable Costs

Many costs are a combination of both the above costs. The total amount in such costs will then change with volume, but not proportionately. It is always best to try and separate this into two components – fixed cost and variable cost, and deal with them separately. For example, telephone bills usually contain a fixed charge for having a connection and a variable charge based on actual usage. In this case, it is easy to separate the two costs. Similarly, the cost of driving a car includes many other cost components, like the cost of gasoline, oil, tires, and maintenance, all of which are variable. But there are also costs of insurance and registration that are fixed. Hence, the total cost in both the above cases is semi-variable and can be easily separated into its fixed and variable components.

The two distinctions of costs – Direct and Indirect and Variable and Fixed are on separate dimensions. Hence, every cost would be a combination of these. The following combinations are possible:

a) **Direct and Variable** – Cost of car tires

b) **Direct and Fixed** – Rent of factory producing only one kind of car

c) **Indirect and Variable** – Cost of power in a factory producing several types of cars

d) **Indirect and Fixed** – Rent of factory producing several types of cars

Unit Costs

Several times costs are quoted on a per-unit basis, like $5 per piece. This means that one piece costs $5. In this case, $5 is a unit cost. However, there are important considerations while computing unit costs.

Firstly, unit costs will remain constant for variable costs. So if the unit variable cost is $5 per piece, it will remain the same even if the volume doubles. But in cases where raw materials can be procured cheaper in bulk and where economies of scale exist, the unit variable cost could reduce. A similar effect can be seen if the volume decreases significantly and volume discounts can no longer be availed of.

Secondly, with the increase in volume, the fixed cost per unit reduces and vice versa; volume and fixed cost per unit are inversely proportional. The total fixed cost remains the same irrespective of volume.

Calculating unit costs by taking all costs into consideration will be misleading. Fixed costs should first be removed from the total costs before unit cost calculations are computed. Below is an example.

Number of units: 1,000

Total Variable cost: $10,000

Total Fixed cost: $50,000

Hence, Unit Variable cost = $10,000/1,000 = $10

Unit Fixed cost = $50,000/1,000 = $50

Total Unit cost = $10 + $50 = $60

Now if the company produces 2,000 units instead of 1,000, then the unit costs will be as below:

Unit Variable cost = $10 (this will not change with number of units)

Unit Fixed cost = $50,000/2,000 = $25

Total Unit cost = $10 + $25 = $35

Total Variable cost = $10 x 2,000 = $20,000

In summary, unit costs should always be computed by first separating fixed costs from variable costs and keeping in mind the effect of volume discounts and economies of scale.

Inventoriable Costs

All costs related to manufacturing that can be inventorized into the company's balance sheet are called inventoriable costs. They fall under the following three categories:

a. **Direct material costs** – Cost of materials required to make the product and whose cost can be traced back to the product

b. **Direct manufacturing labor costs** – Cost of labor required to make the product and whose cost can be traced back to the product

c. **Indirect manufacturing costs** – Overhead costs that cannot be directly traced to the product but are related to the product

All inventoriable costs appear in the company's balance sheet under the item "Inventory" until the products are sold, after which they appear in the company's income statement under the item "Cost of Goods Sold".

Companies can have three types of inventory:

a. **Direct materials inventory** – Inventory of raw materials

b. **Work-in-process inventory** – Inventory of partially manufactured products

c. **Finished goods inventory** – Inventory of ready products that are not yet sold

Consider an example of a pencil manufacturer. They have the following inventory levels:

Direct material (wood and lead) inventory: $500

Work-in-process inventory (including direct and indirect manufacturing costs): $2,000

Finished goods inventory (including direct and indirect manufacturing costs): $5,000

The company would show $7,500 ($500 + $2,000 + $5,000) as inventory in its balance sheet this year. If the company has managed to sell its entire finished goods inventory by next year and there is no other change, then next year's balance sheet will show $2,500 ($500 + $2,000) as inventory and $5,000 will appear in the cost of goods sold in next year's income statement.

Period Costs

All costs that are not inventoriable are period costs. For example, selling costs, marketing costs, R and D costs, and distribution costs. These costs appear under expenses in the income statement. They are not part of the cost of goods sold. They never appear on the balance sheet.

Prime Costs

These are all direct manufacturing costs. They are computed as follows:

Prime costs = Direct material costs + Direct manufacturing labor costs

Conversion Costs

These are the costs incurred in converting the raw materials into finished products. They are computed as given below:

$$Conversion\ costs = Direct\ manufacturing\ labor\ costs + Manufacturing\ overhead\ costs$$

1.2 Using a Costing System

A costing system is used primarily for two purposes – computing total cost incurred by a company, department, or individual products/services and for making decisions using this data.

Cost Computation

As discussed earlier, every company has Direct and Indirect costs. Using these costs, companies compute the Cost of Goods Sold (COGS), which is used for Financial Reporting via Income Statement (refer to chapter "Income Statement" in the book "Financial Accounting Essentials You Always Wanted to Know" of Self-Learning Management Series).

The section below shows how the costing data is used to compute the Cost of Goods Manufactured, which is then used to compute the Cost of Goods Sold. The later chapters explain how Indirect costs are allocated using Activity Based Costing (ABC) and how Support Department costs are allocated.

Cost of Goods Manufactured

As the name suggests, Cost of Goods Manufactured is the cost incurred in manufacturing goods. It includes only inventoriable costs.

The diagram below shows how it is computed:

Figure 1.5

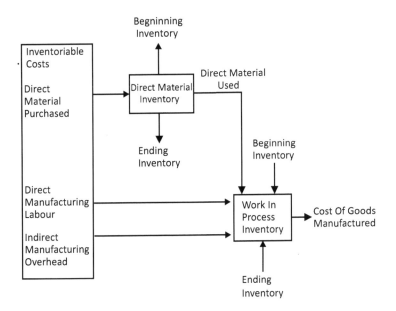

Consider the following example of how Cost of Goods Manufactured is computed using the above diagram. The following values are available for the year for a company:

a) Beginning inventory of Direct Materials = $500

b) Purchase of Direct Materials in the year = $200

c) Ending inventory of Direct Materials = $400

d) Beginning inventory of Work-in-process = $1,000

e) Ending inventory of Work-in-process = $900

f) Direct manufacturing labor for the year = $200

g) Indirect manufacturing overhead for the year = $100

Below are the computations for Cost of Goods Manufactured:

Direct Materials:

Beginning inventory	$500	
Purchase of Direct Materials	$200	
Direct Materials available for use	$700	
Ending inventory	($400)	
Direct Materials used		$300
Direct Manufacturing Labor		$200
Indirect manufacturing overhead		$100
Manufacturing costs incurred		$600
Beginning Work-in-process inventory		$1,000
Total manufacturing costs to account for		$1,600
Ending Work-in-process inventory		($900)
Cost of Goods Manufactured		$700

Cost of Goods Sold

The item Cost of Goods Sold, appears in the Income statement of those companies who have costs that are being reported as inventory until a sale takes place.

The following diagram shows how it is calculated using Cost of Goods Manufactured:

Figure 1.6

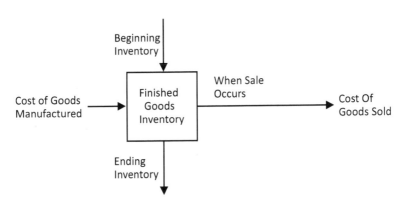

Consider the example in the previous section. Below is some additional information that will help in computing Cost of Goods Sold:

a) Beginning inventory of Finished goods = $400

b) Ending inventory of Finished goods = $600

Below is the computation of Cost of Goods Sold:

Beginning Finished goods inventory	$400
Cost of Goods Manufactured	$700
Cost of Goods available for sale	$1,100
Ending Finished goods inventory	($600)
Cost of Goods Sold	$500

Preparing the Income Statement

The Income Statement contains Cost of Goods Sold and Period costs described above. Consider the example given in the previous section.

Below are the revenue and period costs:

a) Revenue = $1,500

b) R and D cost = $100

c) Marketing cost = $200

d) Customer service cost = $150

Below is the Income Statement:

Revenue		$1,500.00
Cost of Goods Sold		$500.00
Gross Profit		$1,000.00
Operating costs		
R and D	$100.00	
Marketing	$200.00	
Customer service	$150.00	
Total operating costs		$450.00
Operating Income		$550.00

Note that as a convention we do not mention expenses as negative values in the Income Statement. Revenues are always added and expenses are always subtracted while computing Operating Income. With this knowledge, it is much easier to read and understand income statements.

Decision-Making

Costing systems are also used for decision-making. In the next chapter, we will see how costs affect the volume and profit of the company. The following chapter shows how costing systems help in making decisions using relevant information.

Solved Examples

1. A car manufacturer makes five different car models at its plant. Separate assembly lines are used for each model. Classify the various cost items given below into:

   Direct or Indirect

   Variable or Fixed

   Answer with respect to any one car model.

   i.   Annual awards dinner for suppliers

   ii.   Fire insurance policy for the plant

   iii. Cost of tires of the car model

   iv.   Salary of the marketing manager of the plant

   v.   Salary of design engineer of the car model

   vi.   Freight costs of engines from foreign supplier

   vii. Power bill for the entire plant

   viii. Hourly wages paid to temporary workers where each worker works on a single car model

Solution:

   i.   **Annual awards dinner for suppliers** – Indirect and Fixed

         This cost cannot be traced to any particular car model (assuming that suppliers supply parts for multiple car models and there is no clear separation between suppliers of a particular model) and does not vary with manufactured volumes.

ii.   **Fire insurance policy for the plant** – Indirect and Fixed

This also cannot be traced, nor does it vary with volume.

iii. **Cost of tires of the car model** – Direct and Variable

This can be directly traced to the car and varies with the number of cars produced.

iv.   **Salary of the marketing manager of the plant** – Indirect and Fixed

The cost of the marketing manager is shared across all car models, so it cannot be easily traced to one car model. It is also expected that changes in volume should not have any effect on the salary. In reality, however, the marketing manager could be given a bonus that is based on the number of cars sold, or the company may add more managers if the volumes increase a lot. In both cases, the cost may still not be directly proportional to volume but will be more like a chunky step cost.

v.   **Salary of design engineer of the car model** – Direct and Fixed

This cost can be directly traced to the particular car model and is not expected to vary proportionately with volume.

vi.   **Freight costs of engines from foreign supplier** – Direct and Variable

This can be directly attributed to a single car model and has a direct relationship with volume as each car has one engine.

vii. **Power bill for the entire plant** – Indirect and Variable

Since there is a single power bill it cannot be traced to individual models but varies with the volume of production.

viii. **Hourly wages paid to temporary workers** – Direct and Variable

Since each worker works on a particular car model and receives hourly wages, the cost can be directly traced to the car and is directly proportional to the number of cars manufactured.

2. **Using the information given below for AAA Inc., compute the cost of goods manufactured and the income statement for the year. Also, calculate prime and conversion costs.**

Item	Beginning balance	Ending balance
Direct materials inventory	$10,000	$15,000
Work-in-process inventory	$20,000	$18,000
Finished goods inventory	$15,000	$20,000
Direct material purchases		$20,000
Direct manufacturing labor		$3,500
Indirect manufacturing labor		$2,500
Depreciation of plant		$2,000
Insurance of plant		$1,500
Plant maintenance costs		$3,000
Marketing costs		$5,000
Administrative costs		$2,000
Revenue		$50,000

Solution:

From the above information, we can come up with the following inventoriable and period costs. The prior go into the computation of cost of goods manufactured and the latter go into the income statement.

Item	Type of Cost
Direct material purchases	Inventoriable
Direct manufacturing labor	Inventoriable
Indirect manufacturing labor	Inventoriable
Depreciation of plant	Inventoriable
Insurance of plant	Inventoriable
Plant maintenance costs	Inventoriable
Marketing costs	Period
Administrative costs	Period
Plant maintenance costs	
Marketing costs	
Administrative costs	
Revenue	

Below is the computation of cost of goods manufactured:

Direct Materials:

Beginning inventory	$10,000	
Purchase of Direct Materials	$20,000	
Direct Materials available for use	$30,000	
Ending inventory	($15,000)	
Direct Materials used		$15,000
Direct Manufacturing Labor		$3,500

Overhead costs:

Indirect manufacturing labor	$2,500	
Depreciation of plant	$2,000	
Insurance of plant	$1,500	
Plant maintenance costs	$3,000	
Indirect manufacturing overhead		$9,000
Manufacturing costs incurred		$27,500
Beginning Work-in-process inventory		$20,000
Total manufacturing costs to account for		$47,500
Ending Work-in-process inventory		($18,000)
Cost of Goods Manufactured		$29,500

Below is the computation of cost of goods sold:

Beginning Finished goods inventory	$15,000
Cost of Goods Manufactured	$29,500
Cost of Goods available for sale	$44,500
Ending Finished goods inventory	($20,000)
Cost of Goods Sold	$24,500

Below is the Income Statement:

Revenue		$50,000.00
Cost of Goods Sold		$24,500.00
Gross Profit		$25,500.00
Operating costs		
Marketing	$5,000.00	
Administrative	$2,000.00	
Total operating costs		$7,000.00
Operating Income		$18,500.00

Prime costs = Direct material costs + Direct manufacturing labor costs = $15,000 + $3,500 = $18,500

Conversion costs = Direct manufacturing labor costs + Manufacturing overhead costs = $3,500 + $9,000 = $12,500

Practice Exercise

1. A marketing research company organizes customer focus groups for its clients. Those who take part in the survey get paid by the hour for each session. The company has also hired professionals who organize and conduct these sessions. They are paid a fixed salary apart from a variable component for each session that they conduct. Classify the various cost items given below into:

   a. Direct or Indirect

   b. Variable or Fixed

   Below are the costs to be classified:

   i.   Meals provided to participants during the session

   ii.   Rent of company's corporate office

   iii.   Annual subscription charges to marketing research magazines

   iv.   Payment to participants of the session

   v.   Fixed amount paid to professionals who conduct the sessions

   vi.   Telecommunication costs paid in calling participants of focus groups

   vii.   Transportation costs of company's employees who travel for the session

2. **Following is the information available on XYZ Inc. Using this information, prepare a statement of goods manufactured and an income statement. Compute prime and conversion costs.**

Purchase of direct materials	$54,000
Indirect labor	$15,000
Direct labor	$31,200
Depreciation on machinery	$9,000
Sales	$165,90
Selling and administrative expenses	$18,900
Rent on factory building	$21,000

	Inventories	
	Beginning	Ending
Direct materials	$24,000	$26,100
Work-in-process	$6,300	$9,600
Finished goods	$15,000	$17,100

3. **ZZZ Inc. designs office and residential buildings. The following data is available:**

Direct Labor	$600,000
Direct material purchases	$40,000
Administrative costs	$130,000
Overhead costs	$75,000
Selling costs	$265,000
Beginning direct materials inventory	$20,000
Beginning designs in process	$14,000
Ending direct materials inventory	$10,000
Ending designs in process	$39,000

The average design fee is $700 and 2,000 designs were processed during the year.

Compute the cost of goods (designs) manufactured and prepare the income statement.

Solutions to the above questions can be downloaded from the **Online Resources** *section of this book on* **www.vibrantpublishers.com**

Chapter Summary

◆ Accounting Systems can be divided into Financial Accounting System and Managerial Accounting System, used by external decision-makers and internal decision-makers respectively.

◆ Costs can be categorized based on the cost object. Direct costs are traced directly to the cost object, whereas, Indirect costs cannot be directly traced to the cost object. Variable costs vary in direct proportion to the change in the quantity or volume, whereas fixed costs do not. Unit costs contain per unit fixed and per unit variable costs.

◆ All costs related to manufacturing that can be shown in the Balance Sheet are called Inventoriable costs. All non-inventoriable costs are classified as Period costs. All direct manufacturing costs are called Prime costs. The Total cost expended in converting raw materials to finished goods is called Conversion cost.

◆ All Inventoriable costs are included in the Cost of Goods Manufactured. Once the goods are sold from the inventory, those costs are moved into Cost of Goods Sold (COGS). COGS is a term that appears in the Income Statement (P&L statement) of the organization.

◆ The Income statement has revenue on top, from which we subtract the COGS to get Gross Profit. Then we subtract all Period costs to get the Operating Income. Operating Income is a very important figure that helps us in decision making.

This page is intentionally left blank

Chapter 2

Cost-Volume-Profit (CVP) Analysis

This chapter covers the Cost-Volume-Profit Analysis for product decision-making.

The key learning objectives of this chapter are:

- Understand the contribution income statement

- Learn how to use the three levers – Cost, Volume, and Profit, to get maximum profitability

- Understand the concept of breakeven point

- Learn how to use CVP analysis to make decisions

A Cost-Volume-Profit (CVP) analysis examines the behavior of total revenue, total costs, and operating income due to changes in units sold (volume), selling price, variable cost per unit, or fixed cost. This analysis helps make decisions related to the selling price of a product or service or choosing a cost structure from various cost structures that are available. We shall see how it is used later in this chapter.

2.1 Contribution Income Statement

This is a modified form of an Income Statement that is used in CVP analysis. The table below shows the difference:

Regular Income Statement

Revenues	$1,000
Cost of goods sold	$500
Gross profit	$500
Non-manufacturing costs	$200
Operating income	$300

Contribution Income Statement

Revenues		$1,000
Variable manufacturing costs	$200	
Variable non-manufacturing costs	$100	$300
Contribution margin		$700
Fixed manufacturing costs	$300	
Fixed non-manufacturing costs	$100	$400
Operating income		$300

As seen above, both income statements give the same operating income, but the costs are re-arranged to provide different information. The fixed and variable costs are separately mentioned in the Contribution Income Statement to get the Contribution Margin.

Contribution Margin Equations

Operating Income = Revenues – Variable Costs – Fixed Costs

However,

Revenues = Selling Price x Quantity Sold and

Variable Costs = Variable Cost per Unit x Quantity Sold

So,

Operating Income = (Selling Price x Quantity Sold) – (Variable Cost per Unit x Quantity Sold) – Fixed Costs

In terms of Contribution Margin, the above equation can be written as:

Operating Income = (Contribution Margin per Unit x Quantity Sold) – Fixed Costs

Where,

Contribution Margin per Unit = Selling Price – Variable Cost per Unit

Another important measure is the Contribution Margin Percentage given as:

Contribution Margin Percentage = Contribution Margin/Revenue

In the above example, Contribution Margin Percentage = $700/$1,000 = 0.7 or 70%

2.2 CVP Analysis

As we stated earlier, this is the analysis of certain variables (revenue, cost, operating income) due to change in others (volume, variable cost per unit, fixed cost, selling price). Let's look at the effects one by one.

Change in Volume

SP = $100	5 units sold		50 units sold	
Revenues	5 x 100	$500	50 x 100	$5,000
Variable costs	5 x 70	$350	50 x 70	$3,500
Fixed costs		$600		$600
Operating income		($450)		$900

Revenues and operating income change with a change in volume. The variable cost per unit and fixed cost remain the same. In the first case, the company would incur a loss if it sold only five units. This is because the revenues are not enough to cover all the fixed costs.

Change in Selling Price

Volume = 15	SP = $100		SP = $120	
Revenues	15 x 100	$1,500	15 x 120	$1,800
Variable costs	15 x 70	$1,050	15 x 70	$1,050
Fixed costs		$600		$600
Operating income		($150)		$150

Revenues and operating income once again change with a change in the selling price. Other values remain constant. Once again, there could be a loss if the selling price is too low and cannot cover the fixed costs.

Change in Variable cost per Unit

Volume = 20, SP = $100	Var cost/unit = $80		Var cost/unit = $60	
Revenues	20 x 100	$2,000	20 x 100	$2,000
Variable costs	20 x 80	$1,600	20 x 60	$1,200
Fixed costs		$600		$600
Operating income		($200)		$200

A lower variable cost per unit has a favorable impact on the operating income but it does not change the revenues at the fixed volume and selling price.

Change in Fixed Costs

Volume = 40, SP = $100	Fixed costs = $1,000		Fixed costs = $500	
Revenues	40 x 100	$4,000	40 x 100	$4,000
Variable costs	40 x 80	$3,200	40 x 80	$3,200
Fixed costs		$1,000		$500
Operating income		($200)		$300

Change in fixed costs affect operating income only. Everything else remains the same. Hence, fixed costs have a direct impact on the operating income and are a very useful area to take into consideration when trying to reduce costs.

2.3 Breakeven Point and Target Income

The point at which the total revenues are equal to the total costs is called Breakeven Point (BEP). At this point, the operating income is equal to 0. Applying this to the contribution margin equation, we get the following:

Operating Income = 0 = (Contribution Margin per Unit x Quantity Sold) – Fixed Costs

Hence,

Quantity sold at BEP = Fixed Costs/Contribution Margin per Unit

If one needs to find out the quantity to be sold to achieve a certain amount of operating income, then the equation below can be used:

Quantity sold = (Operating Income + Fixed Costs)/Contribution Margin per Unit

Let's take an example. A company needs to find the breakeven point of one of its new products. Below are the available details:

Selling price = $100

Variable cost per unit = $65

Fixed costs = $20,000

We can compute the contribution margin per unit as below:

Contribution margin per unit = $100 - $65 = $35

At BEP, operating income = 0

Hence,

Quantity sold at BEP = Fixed costs/Contribution margin

per unit = $20,000/$35 = 571.43

So the company needs to sell at least 572 units of the product to achieve breakeven.

Now assume, instead, that the company is looking to generate $5,000 from this product and wants to know how much it should sell. Below is the calculation:

Quantity sold = (Operating income + Fixed costs)/Contribution margin per unit

= ($5,000 + $20,000)/$35 = 714.3

Hence, the company needs to sell at least 715 units to achieve the desired operating income.

Tax Effect

If the company is looking for a target Net Income instead of Operating Income, then the effect of tax needs to be considered as below:

Net Income = Operating Income x (1 – Tax rate)

Hence,

$$Operating\ Income = Net\ Income/(1 - Tax\ rate)$$

Below is an example of calculating quantity sold at BEP to achieve a certain Net Income:

Selling Price = $200

Variable cost per unit = $100

Fixed costs = $25,000

Net Income = $20,000

Tax rate = 30%

Operating Income = Net Income/(1 – Tax rate) = $20,000/(1 – 0.3) = $28,571.43

Contribution margin per unit = Selling Price – Variable cost per unit = $200 - $100 = $100

Quantity sold = (Operating income + Fixed costs)/Contribution margin per unit

= ($28,571.43 + $25,000)/$100 = 535.72

Hence, the company would need to sell at least 536 units to achieve the required net income.

2.4 CVP Analysis for Decision Making

As seen above, CVP analysis is used to analyze the effects of several variables on others. Below are some of the areas of decision-making where this analysis helps:

Decision to Advertise

When a company needs to decide on whether it should advertise or not, it can turn to CVP analysis for the answer. The analysis would show whether advertising would increase the operating income or not. If it does, then it is better to advertise. Otherwise, it would be better not to. Let us look at an example.

A company thinks that it can sell 100 units of a product in a convention if it does not advertise. However, if it does advertise, it expects to sell 150 units. The cost of advertising is $15,000. This adds to the other fixed costs of $5,000. The variable cost per unit, other fixed costs and selling price do not change. Below is a comparison of the two situations:

SP = $500, Var cost/unit = $300	Without advertising		With advertising	
Revenues	100 x 500	$50,000	150 x 500	$75,000
Variable costs	100 x 300	$30,000	150 x 300	$45,000
Contribution margin		$20,000		$30,000
Fixed costs		$5,000		$20,000
Operating Income		$15,000		$10,000

As seen from the above comparison, the operating income with advertising is actually lower than it is without advertising. Hence, the company is better off selling lesser without advertising as the additional fixed cost of advertising is not being covered by the additional revenue generated.

Decision to Reduce Selling Price

If the company wants to increase its income by reducing the selling price in order to sell more units, it can use CVP analysis to analyze this change. If the analysis shows that the operating income will increase by selling more units at a lower price, then that option would be preferable. Let's look at an example.

A company can sell 1,000 units of a product at a selling price of $200 but if it reduces the selling price by 20%, it can sell 30% more units. The fixed costs would remain the same in both at $10,000. Variable cost per unit also remains constant at $100.

Below is a comparison:

	SP = $200		SP = $160	
Revenues	1000 x 200	$200,000	1300 x 160	$208,000
Variable costs	1000 x 100	$100,000	1300 x 100	$130,000
Contribution margin		$100,000		$78,000
Fixed costs		$10,000		$10,000
Operating Income		$90,000		$68,000

Once again, the company seems to be in a better position keeping the selling price at $200 as that gives higher operating income even though the volume of products sold is lower.

Decision to Select Cost Structure

When a company has the choice of selecting one of many cost structures, it would choose the one that gives the most operating income. The cost structures would include different levels of fixed and variable costs.

Let's say that a company is planning to keep a stall to sell its products in an electronics expo. The expo rents out stalls with the following alternative payment arrangements:

Alternative 1: $250,000 fixed charge

Alternative 2: $50,000 fixed charge + 2% of revenue earned at the stall

Alternative 3: No fixed charge but 10% of revenue earned at the stall

In order for the company to choose from the above alternatives it needs to undertake a CVP analysis with respect to the following data:

Selling price = $500

Variable cost per unit = $150

Units sold (expected) = 10,000

	Alternative 1		Alternative 2		Alternative 3	
Revenues	10,000 x 500	$5,000,000	10,000 x 500	$5,000,000	10,000 x 500	$5,000,000
Variable costs	10,000 x 150	$1,500,000	10,000 x 150	$1,500,000	10,000 x 150	$1,500,000
Contribution margin		$3,500,000		$3,500,000		$3,500,000
Fixed costs		$250,000		$150,000		$500,000
Operating income		$3,250,000		$3,350,000		$3,000,000

From the above analysis, it is clear that Alternative 2 is the one that would bring the most income to the company and so it should select that option.

The above example has alternatives that differ only in the fixed costs. Degree of Operating Leverage can be used to see the effects of fixed costs on operating income for different units of product sold and contribution margin, as given below:

Degree of Operating Leverage = Contribution Margin/Operating Income

Applying it to the above example gives the following:

	Alternative 1		Alternative 2		Alternative 3	
Revenues	10,000 x 500	$5,000,000	10,000 x 500	$5,000,000	10,000 x 500	$5,000,000
Variable costs	10,000 x 150	$1,500,000	10,000 x 150	$1,500,000	10,000 x 150	$1,500,000
Contribution margin		$3,500,000		$3,500,000		$3,500,000
Fixed costs		$250,000		$150,000		$500,000
Operating income		$3,250,000		$3,350,000		$3,000,000
Operating Leverage		1.08		1.04		1.17

As seen above, the Operating Leverage is lowest for Alternative 2 which has the least fixed cost and highest for Alternative 3 which has the highest fixed cost. Operating leverage is the percentage by which the operating income would change for a 1% change in the revenue or contribution margin. Let's look at how it can be used:

For Alternative 3, a 1% change in revenue would be:

Revenues = $5,000,000 + $50,000 = $5,050,000

This will be for Units = $5,050,000/$500 = 10,100

Below are the calculations:

		Alternative 3
Revenues	10,100 x 500	$5,050,000
Variable costs	10,100 x 150	$1,515,000
Contribution margin		$3,535,000
Fixed costs		$500,000
Operating income		$3,035,000

Change in Operating Income = $3,035,000 - $3,000,000 = $35,000

Percentage change in Operating Income = $35,000/$3,000,000 = 0.0117 or 1.17%

When fixed costs are higher, the degree of Operating Leverage is also higher. This gives a greater incentive to companies to increase their revenues as it adds a greater percentage to the operating income. Having a high degree of operating leverage is neither good nor bad. In most cases, it depends on the industry's typical cost structure. For example, power generation companies have high fixed costs due to huge capital investments and hence have a higher degree of Operating Leverage. Services companies, on the other hand, have a much lower fixed cost, and hence, a lower degree of Operating Leverage.

2.5 Sensitivity Analysis

Knowing that the company would make a profit may sometimes not be enough, as there could be uncertainty in the number of units sold. It may also be useful to know how much risk of running a loss the company is facing.

This is measured by Margin of Safety, given below:

Margin of Safety = Budgeted revenues − Breakeven revenues

Margin of Safety (in units) = Budgeted sales (in units) − Breakeven sales (in units)

It is also represented in a percentage form as below:

Margin of Safety Percentage = Margin of safety/Budgeted revenues

Margin of Safety Percentage gives the percentage by which the revenues should fall in order for the company to start making losses. Below is an example:

Selling Price = $50

Variable costs per Unit = $20

Fixed costs = $20,000

Budgeted units sold = 1,000

Below is the calculation for BEP:

BEP units = Fixed Costs/Contribution Margin per Unit = $20,000/ ($50 - $20) = 667 units

BEP revenues = $50 x 667 = $33,350

Budgeted revenues = $50 x 1,000 = $50,000

Therefore, Margin of Safety = $50,000 - $33,350 = $16,650

Margin of Safety (in units) = 1,000 – 667 = 333 units

Margin of Safety Percentage = $16,650/$50,000 = 33.3%

This means that the revenue needs to fall by 33.3% for the company to start making losses. This looks like a good margin of safety.

CASE STUDY:
Case on Breakeven Point – Fly High

Fly High is an expert in flight bookings for large corporates. It usually charges $1,000 for a round-trip ticket from New York to San Francisco. The commission earned by Fly High is 10% of the ticket price paid by the customer. Fly High incurs a fixed cost of $15,000 per month and a variable cost of $20 per ticket purchased per passenger (when tickets are purchased for multiple passengers, this cost is still incurred per passenger.)

As per the latest changes in the commission structure that is paid by the airlines, they will continue to pay a 10% commission, but with an upper limit of $50 per passenger.

(Assume that Fly High sells only New York San Francisco flight tickets to its customers.)

Case Assignment

i.   As per the earlier commission structure, how many tickets does Fly High need to book to reach a breakeven point?

ii. As per the earlier commission structure, how many tickets does Fly High need to book to earn an operating income of $10,000?

iii. Under the new commission structure, how many more tickets will Fly High need to sell to achieve breakeven?

Solved Examples

1. AAA Inc. manufactures ball pens. It sold 50,000 units last year, each for $20. Variable costs per unit are $11 and total fixed costs are $200,000.

   a. Calculate the contribution margin and operating income.

   b. The company is planning to buy a new machine that would reduce the variable cost to $8 but it will cost $100,000 to procure and install. How does this change the contribution margin and operating income?

   c. Should the new machine be bought?

Solution:

   a. The sheet below shows the contribution margin and operating income:

Revenues	50,000 x 20	$1,000,000
Variable costs	50,000 x 11	$550,000
Contribution margin		$450,000
Fixed costs		$200,000
Operating Income		$250,000

b. The following sheet shows the calculations based on the new machine:

Revenues	50,000 x 20	$1,000,000
Variable costs	50,000 x 8	$400,000
Contribution margin		$600,000
Fixed costs		$300,000
Operating Income		$300,000

c. As seen from the above calculations, the Operating Income increases with the new machine. Hence, the company should buy the new machine.

2. **XYZ Inc. sells airline tickets at a rate of $500 per ticket from LA to San Francisco. It gets a 20% commission on each ticket sold and incurs a $10 variable cost in delivering the tickets to customers. It also has a fixed cost of $100,000 per year.**

   a. **Determine how many tickets the company will need to sell to achieve breakeven.**

   b. **How many more tickets does it need to sell to get an Operating Income of $250,000?**

Solution:

Selling Price = $100 (only 20% of ticket price is the company's revenue)

Variable cost per ticket = $10

Fixed costs = $100,000

Contribution margin per ticket = $100 - $10 = $90

a. Number of tickets at BEP = Fixed costs/Contribution margin per ticket = $100,000/$90 = 1,112

b. Number of tickets to get Operating Income = (Fixed costs + Operating Income)/Contribution margin per ticket

   = ($100,000 + $250,000)/$90 = 3,889

3. **ZZZ Inc. has decided to sell chairs in an exhibition. It will sell each chair at $1,000 which is procured at $700 from a local vendor in bulk. The vendor has agreed to take back any chairs which are not sold. However, he will charge a $10,000 fixed fee for doing so. The company estimates that 100 chairs will be sold.**

   a. **Calculate Operating Income.**

   b. **What is the Degree of Operating Leverage when selling 100 chairs?**

   c. **How much will Operating Income change if revenue increases by 1%?**

Solution:

   a. Below is the calculation of Operating Income:

Revenues	100 x 1,000	$100,000
Variable costs	100 x 700	$70,000
Contribution margin		$30,000
Fixed costs		$10,000
Operating Income		$20,000

   b. Degree of Operating Leverage = Contribution Margin/ Operating Income

      = $30,000/$20,000 = 1.5

   c. Since the degree of operating leverage is 1.5, a 1% increase in revenue will increase the operating income by 1.5%.

Practice Exercise

1. Take a look at the following information:

   Variable Costs = $5,000

   Operating Income = $2,000

   Contribution Margin = $4,000

   Calculate:

   a. Revenues

   b. Fixed Costs

   c. Contribution Margin Percentage

2. AAA Inc. sells vases for $4 each. Following is its cost structure:

Variable costs per unit		
Direct materials	$0.6	
Direct labor	$0.8	
Factory overhead		$0.5
Administrative	$0.3	

Fixed Cost		
Overheads	$9,000	
Marketing		$5000

The company sells 10,000 vases during the year.

Determine the following:

a. What is the company's breakeven point (BEP)?

b. If sales increase by 500 vases, what will be the change in profits?

c. If the tax rate is 40%, how much sales are required to achieve a Net Income of $12,000?

3. ZZZ Inc. has the following Contribution Income Statement for the year:

Sales	$25,000
Variable expenses	$15,000
Contribution Margin	$10,000
Fixed expenses	$4,000
Operating Income	$6,000

a. Calculate the degree of operating leverage

b. If sales increase by 20%, what will be the percentage change in income?

4. XYZ Inc. is planning to rent a place temporarily for selling apparel. It expects to do business only for a month when several tourists are expected due to football matches in the city. It has two options for renting.

Option 1: Fixed rent of $35,000

Option 2: Fixed rent of 10,000 + 5% of sales revenue

The following data is also available:

Average selling price of apparel = $50

Expected volumes to sell = 5,000

Variable cost per apparel = $20

Fixed costs of personnel = $5,000

a. What is the Operating Income for each option?

b. Which of these is a better option?

Solutions to the above questions can be downloaded from the **Online Resources** *section of this book on* **www.vibrantpublishers.com**

Chapter Summary

- We use CVP analysis to show the relationship between product costs, volume, operating profit, fixed costs, variable costs, and pricing. This helps us make a decision.

- The Contribution Income Statement shows variable costs and fixed costs separately. The Contribution margin is the difference between revenue and variable costs. The Operating Income is the difference between contribution margin and fixed costs.

  Operating Income = (Contribution Margin per Unit x Quantity Sold) – Fixed Costs

- An increase only in the volume or selling price always increases the operating income. Reducing the variable costs per unit or total fixed costs also increases operating income.

- Breakeven Point is when operating income is 0.

  Operating Income = 0 = (Contribution Margin per Unit x Quantity Sold) – Fixed Costs

  Quantity sold = (Operating Income + Fixed Costs) / Contribution Margin per Unit

- If the company is looking to target Net Income instead of Operating Income, then tax effects need to be considered

- A Decision to Advertise is beneficial only when the additional fixed costs of advertising are lesser than the increase in revenue due to advertising.

◆ A Reduction in Selling Price is beneficial only if the increased Volume due to price reduction covers the loss of revenue due to price reduction

◆ The Operating Leverage is the percentage by which Operating Income changes for every 1% change in the Revenue. The Operating Leverage increases as the Fixed Cost increases.

Degree of Operating Leverage = Contribution Margin / Operating Income

◆ The Margin of Safety tells us the available cushion, after which loss occurs.

Margin of Safety = Budgeted revenues – Breakeven revenues

Margin of Safety (in units) = Budgeted sales (in units) – Breakeven sales (in units)

Margin of Safety Percentage = Margin of safety / Budgeted revenues

This page is intentionally left blank

Chapter 3

Decision Making using Relevant Information

In this chapter, our focus is to look at making effective decisions by using relevant information.

The key learning objectives of this chapter are:

- Understand how to make decisions based on one-time factors

- Know when to make and when to buy, and the concept of opportunity costs

- Learn to make decisions when you produce multiple products under constraints

When decisions are made about outsourcing, product-mix, or one-time orders, not all costs are relevant. Managers make such decisions using only the relevant costs. Generally, the fixed costs do not change across alternatives and, hence, most often they are not considered while making a decision. Costs and revenue are considered to be relevant only when they meet the following criteria:

a) **Occur in the future** – Only future costs and revenue are relevant. Past costs are called sunk costs and are never relevant in decision-making as they cannot be recovered. The same principle holds for past revenue.

b) **Differ among alternatives** – Only those costs that are different among alternatives are considered for decision-making. As stated above, generally the fixed costs do not change among alternatives and hence are not relevant.

Suppose a company is considering reorganization wherein it would need to lay off some workers. The reorganization itself would have a cost.

The sheet below shows the costs of both the alternatives along with a difference showing the relevant costs.

	Alternative 1	Alternative 2	Difference
	Do not Reorganize	Reorganize	Relevant costs
Revenues	$100,000	$100,000	$0
Costs:			
Direct materials	$20,000	$20,000	$0
Direct labor	$30,000	$20,000	($10,000)
Manufacturing overhead	$10,000	$10,000	$0
Marketing	$15,000	$15,000	$0
Reorganization cost	$0	$5,000	$5,000
Total costs	$75,000	$70,000	($5,000)
Operating Income	$25,000	$30,000	$5,000

In the above sheet, revenues and most of the costs of both alternatives are the same. The only difference is in the Direct labor and Reorganization costs. This is because due to a reduction in workers, the labor cost goes down and the reorganization cost gets added. The difference shows that these are the only relevant items to consider while making this decision. It is quite obvious that Alternative 2 should be selected, as it has a higher Operating Income. This decision is purely based on quantitative factors. But the reorganization would lead to layoffs that could reduce employee morale. This is one of the qualitative factors to consider. The next few sections describe different scenarios of short-term tactical decision-making using relevant information.

3.1 One-Time-Only Special Orders

When a company receives a one-time order from a customer while it has an idle capacity, the company uses relevant information to decide whether to accept the offer or not. It is assumed that this order would not make any long-term difference to the company's business, like other customers asking for a discount, or that the selling price of other customers is affected. The one-time order needs to be a special order that is not expected to recur or have any long-term impact on the company's regular business.

Quantitative Factors

Let's assume that a company making hot plates has a capacity of making 20,000 units but is currently making only 15,000 units for its customers. It receives a one-time-only order from a hotel chain to provide 5,000 hot plates at $425 each. The regular price is $800 per hot plate.

The variable costs are:

Direct materials cost = $350

Direct labor cost = $50

Variable Marketing costs = $50

The fixed costs are:

Fixed Manufacturing costs = $200,000

Fixed marketing costs = $500,000

The variable marketing cost is not expected to increase due to the special order.

   The following sheet shows the company's income statement without the special order.

	Total	Per Unit
Revenues		$12,000,000	$800
Variable costs:			
Direct materials	$5,250,000		$350
Direct labor	$750,000		$50
Marketing	$750,000		$50
Total Variable costs		$6,750,000	
Contribution Margin		$5,250,000	
Fixed costs:			
Manufacturing	$200,000		
Marketing	$500,000		
Total Fixed costs		$700,000	
Operating Income		$4,550,000	

Now, if the company accepts the special order, the company's income statement would look like the sheet below. Both the income statements are shown for side-by-side comparison. The last column gives only the relevant costs.

		Without Special Order		With Special Order		Relevant Costs
		Total	Per Unit	Total	Per Unit	
Revenues		$12,000,000	$800	$14,125,000	$425	$2,125,000
Variable costs:						
Direct materials	$5,250,000		$350	$7,000,000	$350	($1,750,000)
Direct labor	$750,000		$50	$1,000,000	$50	($250,000)
Marketing	$750,000		$50	$750,000	$50	$0
Total Variable costs		$6,750,000		$8,750,000		($2,000,000)
Contribution Margin		$5,250,000		$5,375,000		$125,000
Fixed costs:						
Manufacturing	$200,000			$200,000		$0
Marketing	$500,000			$500,000		$0
Total Fixed costs		$700,000		$700,000		$0
Operating Income		$4,550,000		$4,675,000		$125,000

The relevant costs are the additional revenue (5,000 x $425), Direct materials, and Direct labor costs. The Variable Marketing costs are constant when accepting the special order, and so are all the Fixed costs. Even though the selling price of the special order is much lower than the regular selling price, the company is still able to increase its operating income by accepting the order. Hence, managers making a decision based on only quantitative factors would accept the special order.

Qualitative Factors

The following qualitative factors might also be taken into account before making a decision. These are more long-term and strategic in nature.

a) When companies take one-time-only special orders, they need to ensure that other customers do not ask for that price, as it would reduce the profit margin from their regular business

b) Special orders could lead to overtime work and reduce employee morale

3.2 Make-or-Buy Decisions

When companies need to decide whether to make certain parts themselves or to outsource them, once again, they turn to cost accounting for a quantitative analysis.

Quantitative Factors

Below are the costs of manufacturing a part required in the company's cars:

Direct material costs = $100,000

Direct manufacturing labor = $200,000

Variable manufacturing overheads (setup, utility costs) = $40,000

Fixed manufacturing overheads (lease, rent, insurance costs) = $50,000

They produce 100,000 units of the part.

Below is the total cost of manufacturing the part:

	Total	Per Unit
Direct materials	$100,000	$1.00
Direct manufacturing labor	$200,000	$2.00
Variable manufacturing overheads	$40,000	$0.40
Fixed manufacturing overheads	$50,000	$0.50
Total manufacturing costs	$390,000	$3.90

As seen above, the company incurs $3.9 per part when producing it. Another company offers to sell the same part to the company for $3.6. The company needs to decide whether to outsource production or not. Just looking at the above calculation, it may seem like outsourcing is cheaper. But in order to make the decision, only relevant costs should be taken into account as shown below:

	Make		Buy	
	Total	Per Unit	Total	Per Unit
Procurement cost			$360,000	$3.60
Direct materials	$100,000	$1.00		
Direct manufacturing labor	$200,000	$2.00		
Variable manufacturing overheads	$40,000	$0.40		
Total relevant costs	$340,000	$3.40	$360,000	$3.60

In the above analysis, we have omitted the Fixed manufacturing overheads, as they are expected to stay even though the work is outsourced. The only relevant costs are the variable costs in this case. Hence, the company is better off making the part.

Qualitative Factors

The following qualitative factors could apply to make-or-buy decisions:

- Companies might decide to make instead of buy to retain control over production, even though outsourcing is cheaper.

- Companies may prefer to outsource even though it is costlier, in order to concentrate on their core competencies. This means that outsourcing could be costlier, but the company would like to concentrate on other areas of business that could add value in the future.

- The outsourcing decision may not always be based on cost. Companies look at the quality of products and try to maintain a long-term relationship with suppliers to avoid delays in the delivery schedules.

3.3 Outsourcing and Opportunity Costs

In the above example, the company decides not to go for outsourcing, assuming that the released capacity would not be used for any other purpose. However, if the company is able to rent out the premises to someone else or use the capacity to manufacture something else, then that additional revenue needs to be considered before making a decision based on the quantitative analysis. The cost associated with the lost opportunity of using the premises for some other purpose is called Opportunity Cost.

Let's say that in the above example, the company is able to rent out its premises to another company for a rent of $70,000. This amount is called the opportunity cost. It is the loss of revenue or opportunity of selecting an alternative. This amount can be either subtracted from the total costs of alternative 2 or added to the total costs of alternative 1. We shall add it to the total costs of alternative 1. Then the analysis would look like this:

	Make		Buy	
	Total	Per Unit	Total	Per Unit
Procurement cost			$360,000	$3.60
Opportunity cost (of renting)	$70,000	$0.70		
Direct materials	$100,000	$1.00		
Direct manufacturing labo	$200,000	$2.00		
Variable manufacturing overheads	$40,000	$0.40		
Total relevant costs	$410,000	$4.10	$360,000	$3.60

Now, from the above analysis, it is clear that the alternative to buy from outside is better. Similarly, suppose the company is able to use the premises for producing something else rather than renting. The incremental revenues and costs would be as shown below:

	Total
Incremental Revenues	$500,000
Incremental Costs	$400,000
Incremental Operating Income	$100,000

The new part that is produced will bring in an incremental revenue of $500,000 at an additional incremental cost of $400,000. This gives an incremental operating income of $100,000. Below is the comparison of the two alternatives:

	Make		Buy	
	Total	Per Unit	Total	Per Unit
Procurement cost			$360,000	$3.60
Opportunity cost (of making other part)	$100,000	$1.00		
Direct materials	$100,000	$1.00		
Direct manufacturing labor	$200,000	$2.00		
Variable manufacturing overheads	$40,000	$0.40		
Total relevant costs	$440,000	$4.40	$360,000	$3.60

3.4 Product-Mix Decisions with Capacity Constraints

Most companies produce more than one product or service. They may also have constraints in their production. For example, if a company makes two different car models using the same assembly line, the assembly line would become a constraint if it is unable to produce enough units that can be sold. Hence, they need to decide on the appropriate product-mix. Capacity constraints do not allow the companies to produce everything they can sell. They need to select the product-mix that maximizes their operating income.

Shown below is an example of a company producing two products:

	Product 1	Product 2
Selling Price	$100	$120
Variable cost per unit	$70	$76
Contribution margin per unit	$30	$44
Contribution margin percentage	30.00%	36.67%

Simply by looking at the above information, the company might decide to produce only Product 2. But due to capacity constraints, the company also needs to look at how much of the capacity-constrained resource is being used by the two products before deciding. Below is the information on how much each product uses the machine that has constrained capacity:

	Product 1	Product 2
Contribution margin per unit	$30	$44
Machine hours on capacity-constrained machine	2	4
Contribution margin per machine hour	$15	$11

From the above analysis, it is clear that a larger amount of Product 1 can be produced by the company, which gives the company a greater contribution margin. Hence, it should produce more of Product 1.

CASE STUDY:
Case on Decision Making using Relevant Information – Mastif Inc.

Mastif Inc. has received a proposal to replace all its current personal computers in the office with laptops that contain the latest hardware and software. Here is the data available.

	Personal Computers	Laptops
Original cost	$45,000	$20,000
Useful life	5 years	3 years
Current age	2 years	-
Remaining useful life	3 years	3 years
Accumulated depreciation	$20,000	-
Current book value	$25,000	-
Current disposable value	$15,000	-
Disposable value 3 years from now	0	0
Annual computer-related operating costs	$6,000	$1,500
Annual revenues	$150,000	$150,000
Annual noncomputer-related operating costs	$125,000	$125,000

Case Assignment

i. Compare the operating income of continuing with the personal computers with the operating income of replacing them with laptops over 3 years. (Ignore the time value of money and taxes.)

ii. What decision should Mastif Inc. take?

iii. If the management of Mastif Inc. is given a yearly bonus based on the yearly operating income, would the decision remain the same? (Hint: Compute the operating income for the 1st year for comparison)

Solved Examples

1. **XYZ Inc. has received a proposal from its mechanical department to replace an old machine. The following data shows details of the current and new machines:**

	Current machine	New machine
Original cost	$2,000,000	$900,000
Useful Life (in years)	5	3
Used Life (in years)	2	0
Accumulated depreciation	$800,000	$0
Current disposal value	$600,000	$0
Terminal disposal value (after 3 years)	$0	$0
Annual operating costs	$100,000	$50,000
Annual maintenance costs	$40,000	$40,000
Annual revenues	$2,000,000	$2,000,000

Should the company replace the current machine?

Solution:

In order to decide between the two alternatives, the company needs to calculate the operating income of the two alternatives. However, if only one year's operating income is taken into account, then the analysis would be incomplete. Instead, the operating income over three years (life of the new machine/ useful life of the current machine is three years) should be taken into account. Below is the analysis:

Analysis for 3 years	Alternative 1 No replacement		Alternative 2 Do replacement	
Revenues	$2,000,000 x 3	$6,000,000	$2,000,000 x 3	$6,000,000
Costs:				
Operating costs	$100,000 x 3	$300,000	$50,000 x 3	$150,000
Maintenance costs	$40,000 x 3	$120,000	$40,000 x 3	$120,000
Remaining Depreciation	$2,000,000 - $800,000	$1,200,000	Full cost of machine	$900,000
Current disposal value	This is not a cost	$0	Will reduce the cost	($600,000)
Terminal disposal value		$0		$0
Total costs		$1,620,000		$570,000
Operating Income		$4,380,000		$5,430,000

The Operating Income over three years from Alternative 2 is higher than Alternative 1. Hence, Alternative 2 should be selected.

2. **ZZZ Inc. produces notebooks. They have the capacity to produce 10,000 units each month. Their current sales are 8,000 units. Their price per notebook is $50. Below are their current costs:**

Direct materials	$80,000
Direct manufacturing labor	$40,000
Variable manufacturing costs	$40,000
Fixed manufacturing labor	$60,000
Fixed marketing costs	$25,000

Another company urgently needs 2,000 notebooks and asks ZZZ Inc. to sell them at $25 per notebook. This is a one-time-only special order without any long-term consequences. Should ZZZ Inc. accept the offer?

Solution:

The company has two alternatives. The first one is to not accept the special order and the other one is to accept the offer at $25 per piece. Below is the analysis of each alternative:

	Without Special order		With Special order
	Total	Per Unit	Total
Revenues	$400,000	$50	$450,000
Variable Costs:			
Direct materials	$80,000	$10	$100,000
Direct manufacturing labor	$40,000	$5	$50,000
Variable manufacturing costs	$40,000	$5	$50,000
Contribution margin	$240,000	$30	$250,000
Fixed Costs:			
Fixed manufacturing labor	$60,000		$60,000
Fixed marketing costs	$25,000		$25,000
Operating Income	$155,000		$165,000

From the above analysis we find that the company can receive a higher Operating Income by accepting the special order.

3. AAA Inc. makes two products – P1 and P2. The following are prices and costs of the two products:

	P1	P2
Selling Price	$50	$20
Costs:		
Direct material	$10	$5
Direct labor	$7	$2
Variable manufacturing	$5	$1
Fixed manufacturing	$5	$2
Fixed marketing	$8	$3
Total Costs	$35	$13
Operating Income	$15	$7

The company uses the same production process to produce both the products, and it does not have enough capacity to meet the demand." Hence, the company needs to decide which product to produce more. P1 takes 1 hour of the production process, whereas, P2 takes 20 minutes of the process. Which product should the company choose to produce?

Solution:

The company has a capacity constraint – the production process. The company should not choose operating income as the criteria to select which product to produce. It should choose the contribution margin per hour of the production process as fixed costs are irrelevant in decision making (they are going to be the same for both alternatives).

Below is the calculation:

	P1	**P2**
Selling Price	$50	$20
Variable Costs::		
Direct material	$10	$5
Direct labor	$7	$2
Variable manufacturing	$5	$1
Total Variable costs	$22	$8
Contribution margin	$28	$12
Use of production process (in hours)	1.00	0.33
Contribution margin per hour of constrained resource	$28	$36

As seen above, even though the contribution margin of P2 is much lower, its contribution margin per hour of the production process (the constraint) is much higher than P1. Hence, the company should produce only P2 as long as they can sell all that they produce. Any time left in the production process can then be devoted to producing P1.

Practice Exercise

1. Which of the following costs are relevant for decision-making when there are two alternatives?

   a. Cost of equipment that is bought in Alternative 2

   b. Operating costs that are same for Alternatives 1 and 2

   c. Cost of equipment bought last year

   d. Fixed costs that will be incurred

   e. Depreciation of equipment that is kept in Alternative 1 and sold in Alternative 2

2. AAA Inc. currently buys 30,000 units of a part used to manufacture its product at $40 per unit. Recently the supplier informed that a 20% increase in price will come into effect next year. AAA has some additional space and could produce the units for the following per-unit costs:

Direct materials	$16
Direct labor	$12
Variable overhead	$12
Fixed overhead (based on 30,000 units)	$10

   If the units are purchased from the supplier, $200,000 of fixed costs will still be incurred. In addition, the plant can be rented out for $20,000 per year if the parts are purchased externally.

   Should the company buy the parts or make them?

3. XYZ Inc. manufactures a product with the following unit costs for 5,000 units:

Direct materials	$60
Direct labor	$30
Factory overhead (40% variable)	$90
Selling expenses (60% variable)	$30
Administrative expenses (20%variable)	$15

Recently a company approached XYZ Inc. to buy 1,000 units of the product for $225. Currently, it is sold for $412.50 to dealers. XYZ Inc. has enough capacity to produce the extra units. No additional selling expenses would be incurred on the special order.

a) Calculate the profit currently earned by the company

b) Should the company accept the special order?

Chapter Summary

◆ For decision making, we use only those revenues and costs that are relevant – i.e., ones that occur in the future and are different from alternatives. Along with quantitative factors, there could be several qualitative factors that also need to be considered.

◆ A one-time-only special order can be accepted if it increases the company's operating income. Qualitative factors that come into the picture are discounts that may be asked by other customers and low employee morale due to overtime work.

◆ When making a make-or-buy decision, we look at the relevant costs and select the alternative with lower costs. Qualitative factors to be considered are retention of control over production, concentration on core competency, quality of product, and long-term relationships with suppliers.

◆ The cost associated with the lost opportunity of using the premises for some other purpose is called Opportunity Cost.

◆ When making a decision on Product Mix, one should look at the contribution margin of the constrained resource for each product type, instead of looking at the contribution margin per unit for each product type.

Chapter 4

Activity-Based Costing

In this chapter, we take a detailed look at how product/service costs are obtained using an activity-based costing system.

The key learning objectives of this chapter are:

- Understand the issues faced when activity-based costing is not used

- Know how to use activity-based costing for accurate costing

- Learn the concept of customer profitability

All companies have Direct and Indirect costs. Companies having only one product or service can allocate all indirect costs to it. However, companies having multiple products or services would need to allocate such costs on some other basis. In this chapter, we will see how indirect costs are allocated to products using individual activities instead of simple averaging.

4.1 Broad Averaging

Companies may decide to simply allocate all costs by averaging them across products. This approach leads to inaccurate costing and may result in product under-costing or product over-costing.

For example, consider four friends going out for dinner. They incur the following costs:

Table 4.1

	Bob	Peter	Lisa	Julie	Total	Average
Starters	$10	$5	$2	$0	$17	$4.25
Main course	$20	$35	$30	$25	$110	$27.50
Drinks	$5	$15	$10	$10	$40	$10
Dessert	$0	$5	$10	$8	$23	$5.75
Total	$35	$60	$52	$43	$190	$47.50

Now if the friends decide to split the bill based on the broad average of $47.50, then Bob and Julie would be paying more than they should, whereas, Peter and Lisa would pay less. Now, this might not be such a bad thing if they are close friends, but it could lead to incorrect decisions in a company. Companies might take incorrect pricing decisions that are based on broad averages and may even decide to continue or discontinue the wrong product line or service. Such a situation is called product-cost cross-subsidization.

4.2 Simple Costing System

A simple costing system is based on the broad averaging of costs described above. All indirect costs are allocated to a single indirect-cost pool and then allocated to the cost object using a single cost-allocation base. This is shown in the diagram below:

Figure 4.1

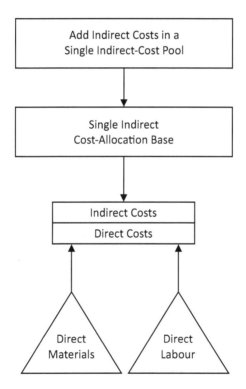

The selection of the cost-allocation base is based on a direct parameter, like direct manufacturing labor hours, total direct manufacturing costs, etc. Once that is selected, all indirect costs are allocated using that base to all products or services (the cost objects). All direct costs are traced directly to the cost objects.

Consider the example of a company that manufactures CD players for cars. It has two models, CD2005 and CD2010. CD2005 is a plain old CD player and is cheaper. CD2010 is a new breed of CD player that can play multiple formats – audio CD, MP3, etc. The company sells these two players to a car manufacturer for $50 and $120 per player respectively. The car manufacturer has recently identified another company that is able to provide players of type CD2005 at $40. Hence, the company now needs to decide whether to reduce the price of its CD2005 player or discontinue selling that model if it is unable to match the cost structure of the competitor. Luckily, it does not have too much competition in the CD2010 market right now.

The company sells 50,000 pieces of CD2005 and 20,000 pieces of CD2010 per year. Its total indirect costs are $1,000,000. It decides to use direct manufacturing labor hours as the cost-allocation base to allocate the indirect costs to the two cost objects – CD2005 and CD2010. The direct manufacturing labor hours for CD2005 are 15,000 and that of CD2010 are 10,000. Hence, the indirect cost per cost-allocation base (direct manufacturing labor hour) is:

Indirect cost per direct manufacturing labor hour = $1,000,000/25,000 = $40

Further, assume the following:

Direct materials cost for producing 50,000 CD2005 = $1,000,000

Direct materials cost for producing 20,000 CD2010 = $1,000,000

Direct manufacturing labor cost for producing 50,000 CD2005 = $400,000

Direct manufacturing labor cost for producing 20,000 CD2010 = $200,000

Below are the cost calculations for both products:

	CD2005		CD2010	
	Total	**Per Unit**	**Total**	**Per Unit**
Direct materials	$1,000,000	$20.00	$1,000,000	$50.00
Direct manufacturing labor	$400,000	$8.00	$200,000	$10.00
Total direct costs	$1,400,000	$28.00	$1,200,000.00	$60.00
Indirect cost allocated ($40x15,000, $40x10,000)	$600,000	$12.00	$400,000	$20.00
Total cost	$2,000,000	$40.00	$1,600,000.00	$80.00
Selling Price		$50.00		$120.00
Operating margin		20%		33%

The company has done the allocation as per the diagram below:

Figure 4.2

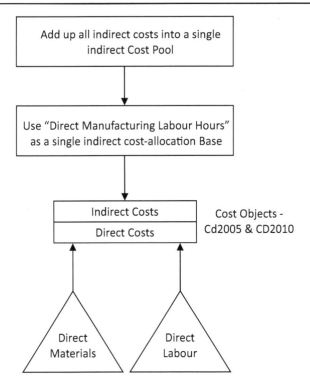

Decision Making

As seen from the above calculations, the company has a lower margin in CD2005 and higher in CD2010. By looking at this information, the company may think that it is not profitable to sell CD2005 for $40 and might decide to forego that business and concentrate on the more profitable product – CD2010.

4.3 Activity-Based Costing System

Activity-Based Costing (ABC) is a system in which all indirect costs are first put into different pools based on the activities performed for the cost being incurred. In the next stage, each indirect-cost pool is allocated to the cost objects using its own indirect cost-allocation base. In effect, it has two differences compared to the simple costing system:

a) Indirect costs are put in separate pools of activities

b) Allocation of indirect costs is done using separate cost-allocation bases

Below is the diagram showing an ABC system:

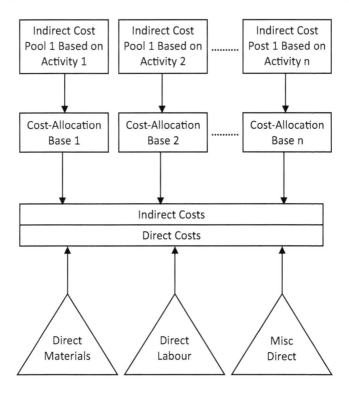

Figure 4.3

Apart from the multiple indirect cost-pools and cost-allocation bases, an ABC system also attempts to try and identify those costs that may seem indirect but are incurred only on a single product or service. In such cases, they can be directly traced back to the cost object and they become a direct cost. Such costs are shown in the diagram as "Misc Direct".

Let's use the ABC system to analyze the cost structure of the company making CD2005 and CD2010 in the above example. But in order to do so, we need additional information on how the indirect costs are incurred – i.e., using which activities. The following information is available:

Activity	Budgeted Cost	Cost-allocation Base	Budgeted Quantity of cost-allocation Base	Indirect Cost Rate
Machine setup	$200,000	Direct	-	-
Distribution	$150,000	CD volume	200	$750
Design	$500,000	CD size	500	$1,000
Administration	$150,000	Direct manufacturing labor hours	25,000	$6
Total	$1,000,000			

The total indirect cost is divided into four activities. Machine setup is an activity that can be directly traced back to the particular CD model, as they use different machines. Hence, it has been converted to a direct cost. The distribution activity can be allocated using the volume of CD, as the volume determines the amount that needs to be delivered. The design activity has CD size as the cost-allocation base, as a bigger size requires more design effort. Finally, administration is best allocated using direct manufacturing labor hours.

The sheet below shows the costs using the ABC system:

	CD2005		CD2010	
	Total	**Per Unit**	**Total**	**Per Unit**
Direct materials	$1,000,000	$20.00	$1,000,000	$50.00
Direct manufacturing labor	$400,000	$8.00	$200,000	$10.00
Machine setup (direct cost based on number of setups)	$50,000	$1.00	$150,000	$7.50
Total direct costs	$1,450,000.00	$29.00	$1,350,000.00	$67.50
Distribution				
CD2005 - $750 x 50 cubic feet volume	$37,500.00	$0.75		
CD2010 - $750 x 150 cubic feet volume			$112,500.00	$5.63
Design				
CD2005 - $1,000 x 180 sq. feet	$180,000.00	$3.60		
CD2010 - $1,000 x 320 sq. feet			$320,000.00	$16.00
Administration				
CD2005 - $6 x 15,000 hr	$90,000	$1.80		
CD2010 - $6 x 10,000 hr			$60,000	$3.00
Total cost	$1,757,500.00	$35.15	$1,842,500.00	$92.13
Selling Price		$50.00		$120.00
Operating margin		30%		23%

The company has undertaken allocation as per the diagram below:

Figure 4.4

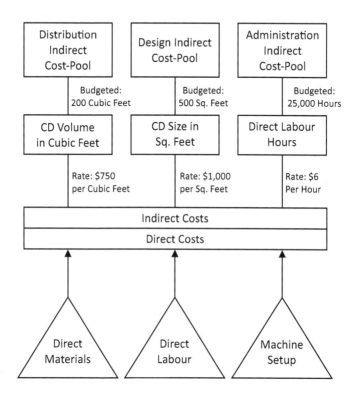

Decision Making

When the costs are allocated using ABC, it turns out that CD2005 is actually more profitable than CD2010. Even if the company wants to reduce the selling price to $40 for meeting the competitor's price, it will still make a profit.

4.4 Customer Profitability

Activity-based costing is very useful in analyzing customer profitability. It is the difference between the revenues earned from a customer and the costs incurred in serving the customer. Sometimes, companies are unaware of their most profitable customers and their least profitable ones or even loss-making accounts. With this knowledge, the company can decide how much effort should be put into which account, in order to increase the overall profitability of the company.

Consider a company that has four customers with the following customer revenues:

Table 4.2

	Customers			
	A	**B**	**C**	**D**
Products sold	40,000	30,000	3,000	2,000
Listed selling price	$150	$150	$150	$150
Discount	$10	$5	$12	$0
Invoicing price	$140	$145	$138	$150
Cost of goods sold	$120	$120	$120	$120

If the company wants to find out which of these four customers are the most and least profitable, it also needs to know the indirect costs associated with each of them. The table below provides this information on the basis of an activity-based accounting system:

Table 4.3

Activity	Rate	Cost driver
Storage	$5	Per product sold
Order handling	$500	Per purchase order
Delivery	$10	Per mile of delivery
Urgent delivery	$2,000	Per urgent delivery, irrespective of distance travelled
Sales cost	$1,000	Per salesperson visit

Below are the actual usages of the above activities per customer:

Table 4.4

	Customers			
	A	B	C	D
Number of Purchase Orders	30	20	15	10
Number of deliveries	50	20	20	10
Average miles per delivery	10	10	20	5
Number of urgent deliveries	2	1	2	0
Number of salesperson visits	5	5	3	2

Using the above information, the company can compute how much cost is associated with each customer and compute the customer profitability in this way:

	Customers			
	A	**B**	**C**	**D**
Revenues				
$140 x 40,000				
$145 x 30,000				
$138 x 3,000				
$150 x 2,000	$5,600,000	$4,350,000	$414,000	$300,000
Cost of goods sold				
$120 x 40,000				
$120 x 30,000				
$120 x 3,000				
$120 x 2,000	$4,800,000	$3,600,000	$360,000	$240,000
Gross margin	$800,000	$750,000	$54,000	$60,000
Storage costs				
$5 x 40,000				
$5 x 30,000				
$5 x 3,000				
$5 x 2,000	$200,000	$150,000	$15,000	$10,000
Order handling costs				
$500 x 30				
$500 x 20				
$500 x 15				
$500 x 10	$15,000	$10,000	$7,500	$5,000
Delivery costs				
$10 x 50 x 10				
$10 x 20 x 10				
$10 x 20 x 20				
$10 x 10 x 5	$5,000	$2,000	$4,000	$500

Urgent delivery costs

$2,000 x 2

$2,000 x 1

$2,000 x 2

$2,000 x 0	$4,000	$2,000	$4,000	$0

Salesperson costs

$1,000 x 5

$1,000 x 5

$1,000 x 3

$1,000 x 2	$5,000	$5,000	$3,000	$2,000
Total indirect costs	$229,000	$169,000	$33,500	$17,500
Operating Income	$571,000	$581,000	$20,500	$42,500
Operating margin	10.20%	13.36%	4.95%	14.17%

As seen from the above analysis, customer D is the most profitable and customer C is least profitable. This is because the indirect costs of customer C are too high for the volume of business it gives to the company. Using this information, the company can focus on customers B and D as they are the most profitable and reduce costs in serving customers C and A.

CASE STUDY:
Case on ABC – Food4Less

Food4Less sells various items in its chain of grocery stores. It is thinking of expanding its reach to adjoining states. In this regard, it wants to select which products to carry in these new stores, as they are smaller in size and cannot carry all products. The profitability of three products is to be calculated in this regard – sodas, veggies, and ready-to-eat foods.

	Sodas	Veggies	Ready-to-eat
Revenue	$50,000	$120,000	$70,000
COGS	$35,000	$86,000	$52,000
Cost for returning bottles	$68	-	-
Number of orders placed	100	350	110
Number of deliveries received	90	900	200
Hours of shelf-stocking time	200	2,000	1,000
Units sold	720	6,300	1,750

The following information is also available from Food4Less from the previous year:

Activity	Description	Support Costs	Cost-allocation Base
Returning bottles	Sending back empty bottles to the distributor	$650	Direct tracing to sodas
Order	Placing orders with distributor	$5,500	560 orders placed
Delivery	Receipt of orders from distributor	$10,000	1,190 deliveries received
Stocking	Shelf stocking of items in the store	$8,000	3,200 hours of shelf-stocking time
Support	Help provided to customers in the store	$11,000	8,770 units sold

Case Assignment

i. Calculate the operating income and operating income margin for each product, assuming that the support costs are allocated based on the cost of goods sold of each product.

ii. Calculate the operating income and operating income margin for each product, assuming that the support costs are allocated based on an ABC system.

iii. Based on the findings from the previous two calculations, what would be your recommendation if Food4Less needs to drop one product line from its new, smaller stores?

Solved Examples

1. AAA Inc. makes two types of bikes – regular and premium. Each bike has its own distribution channel. The total cost of distribution is $4,260,000. Below are some other details that are available:

Type	Number of Distributors	Number of Bikes
Regular	10	240,000
Premium	30	160,000

Currently, the company allocates distribution costs on the basis of the number of bikes shipped. In order to better understand its costs, the company identifies the following activities and related costs:

i. Marketing costs - $16,000 per distributor

ii. Order handling costs - $600 per order. A distributor of regular bikes places on average 10 orders per year and a distributor of premium bikes places 20 orders per year.

iii. Delivery costs - $8 per bike

a. Calculate the total distribution costs and per bike cost for regular and premium bikes using the current costing system of the company.

b. Use the ABC system to derive the above costs.

c. How can the ABC system help change the product decisions of the company?

Solution:

a. Total distribution cost = $4,260,000

Distribution cost per bike = $4,260,000/(240,000 + 160,000)

= $10.65 per bike

Below are the total distribution costs for each category of bikes:

	Regular		Premium	
	Total	Per Unit	Total	Per Unit
Distribution costs				
$10.65 x 240,000				
$10.65 x 160,000	$2,556,000.00	$10.65	$1,704,000.00	$10.65

b. If ABC system is used, the distribution costs would be allocated to multiple indirect-cost pools – marketing, order handling and delivery. Then, the costs would be allocated to the two products using three different cost-allocation bases. Here is the calculation:

	Regular		Premium	
	Total	Per Unit	Total	Per Unit
Marketing costs	$160,000.00	$0.67	$480,000.00	$3.00
$16,000 x 10				
$16,000 x 30				
Order handling costs	$60,000.00	$0.25	$360,000.00	$2.25
$600 x 10 x 10				
$600 x 20 x 30				
Delivery costs				
$8 x 240,000	$1,920,000.00	$8.00	$1,280,000.00	$8.00
$8 x 160,000				
Total Indirect costs	$2,140,000.00	$8.92	$2,120,000.00	$13.25

c. Below is a comparison of the allocation of distribution costs to the two products based on the two different costing systems:

Type	Current system	ABC system
Regular	$10.65	$8.92
Premium	$10.65	$13.25

Using the costing information from the ABC system, the company knows that the Indirect costs of the Regular bikes are lower than those of the Premium bikes. It can use this information to make decisions, like selecting a product-mix of higher profitability and trying to reduce costs at the appropriate places (for example, trying to reduce the marketing and order handling costs of Premium bikes, as these seem much higher than the Regular bikes).

2. **ZZZ Inc. is a retailer selling men's shirts, women's shirts, and unisex t-shirts. Following are the activities it identifies as indirect-cost pools:**

Ordering $1,000 per purchase order

Delivery $800 per delivery

Shelf-stocking $200 per hour

Billing $2 per item sold

Following are the various revenues, costs, and activity usage of each product line:

	Men's Shirts	Women's Shirts	Unisex
Revenue	$550,000	$650,000	$500,000
Cost of goods sold	$350,000	$450,000	$350,000
Support costs (non-ABC)	$105,000	$135,000	$105,000
Activity details:			
Purchase orders	30	25	15
Deliveries	100	30	25
Shelf-stocking hours	200	175	50
Items sold	15,000	20,000	10,000

a. **Using the support costs, without an ABC costing system (non-ABC support costs) find out the operating income of each product line.**

b. **Using the ABC system, compute the operating income of each product line.**

c. **How can the company use this information to make an improvement?**

Solution:

a. Below is the income statement per product using non-ABC cost system:

	Gents Shirts	Ladies Shirts	Unisex T-Shirts
Revenue	$550,000	$650,000	$500,000
Cost of goods sold	$350,000	$450,000	$350,000
Gross profit	$200,000	$200,000	$150,000
Support costs	$105,000	$135,000	$105,000
Operating Income	$95,000	$65,000	$45,000
Operating margin	17.27%	10.00%	9.00%

b. When the ABC system is used, the support costs can be
    allocated using the four indirect-cost allocation bases
    identified. They will be allocated to individual products
    using the cost-allocation bases as below:

	Gents Shirts	Ladies Shirts	Unisex T-Shirts
Revenue	$550,000	$650,000	$500,000
Cost of goods sold	$350,000	$450,000	$350,000
Gross profit	$200,000	$200,000	$150,000
Ordering costs			
$1,000 x 30	$30,000		
$1,000 x 25		$25,000	
$1,000 x 15			$15,000
Delivery costs			
$800 x 100	$80,000		
$800 x 30		$24,000	
$800 x 25			$20,000
Shelf-stocking costs			
$200 x 200	$40,000		
$200 x 175		$35,000	
$200 x 50			$10,000
Billing cost			
$2 x 15,000	$30,000		
$2 x 20,000		$40,000	
$2 x 10,000			$20,000
Total indirect costs	$180,000	$124,000	$65,000
Operating Income	$20,000	$76,000	$85,000
Operating margin	3.64%	11.69%	17.00%

c. By looking at the ABC costing calculations, the company would find that Unisex T-Shirts are the most profitable product line and Men's Shirts are the least. It can then try to increase its sales of Unisex T-Shirts and try to reduce some costs incurred on Men's Shirts. The delivery costs of Gents Shirts seem to be especially high due to more deliveries. It can try to reduce the number of deliveries to cut that cost.

Practice Exercise

1. AAA Inc. has two categories of overheads – maintenance and inspection. The projected costs for these categories for the coming year are as follows:

   Maintenance: $360,000

   Inspection: $750,000

   The plant currently applies overheads using direct labor hours and the expected capacity is 100,000 direct labor hours. The following data has been assembled for use in developing a bid for a proposed job. Bid prices are calculated as full manufacturing cost plus a 20% mark-up.

Direct materials	$2,100
Direct labor	$5,625
Machine hours	450
Direct labor hours	4
Direct labor hours	550

   The total expected machine hours for all jobs during the year are 60,000 and the total expected number of inspections is 4,000.

   a. Compute the total cost of the potential job using direct labor hours to assign overhead. Determine the bid price for the potential job.

   b. Compute the total cost of the job using activity-based costing and the appropriate activity drivers. Determine the bid price if activity-based costing is used.

2. **XYZ Inc. produces two types of watches – low-end and high-end. Data related to the two products is given below:**

	Low-end	High-end
Production	50,000	100,000
Direct materials costs	$150,000	$300,000
Direct labor costs	$75,000	$175,000
Direct manufacturing labor hours	3,000	4,500
Machine hours	10,000	18,000
Number of lots produced	100	100
Inspection effort (hours)	500	750

The combined manufacturing overhead costs are as follows:

Machining costs	$400,000
Setup costs (depend on lots produced)	$100,000
Inspection costs	$100,000

a. **Compute the manufacturing overhead costs per unit for each product.**

b. **Compute the manufacturing cost per unit for each product.**

c. **If the company uses a mark-up of 30%, compute the selling price for each product.**

d. **Identify the main cost drivers for each product. How can the company reduce the costs of manufacturing each product?**

3. ZZZ Inc. distributes medicines to pharmacists and doctors. Following are the activities:

Activity	Rate
Taking order	$400 per order
Billing	$30 per item in order
Delivering order	$500 per delivery
Packaging	$10 per package
Stocking	$150 per hour

The customer profitability of the two customers is to be computed using the data below:

	Pharmacist	Doctor
Total orders	10	10
Average items per order	15	20
Total deliveries	5	10
Average packages per delivery	20	15
Average stocking time per delivery	1 hour	1.5 hours
Number of lots produced	100	100
Inspection effort (hours)	500	750

a. Compute the Operating Income per customer.

b. Comment on the findings and suggest steps to improve customer profitability.

Chapter Summary

♦ Broad averaging of Indirect Costs could lead to under-costing or over-costing of products. In a company with several products, this could lead to cross-subsidization. This can lead to incorrect decision-making regarding the volume, costing, and pricing of products.

♦ A simple costing system uses a single cost-allocation base, which could be erroneous, as it is based on broad averaging.

♦ When using an Activity-Based Costing system (ABC system), all indirect costs are divided into separate pools of activities, and separate cost-allocation bases are used to distribute them to the various products. This system provides the most accurate costing figure for indirect costs, and hence provides good quality data for decision-making.

♦ Activity-Based Costing is also useful in calculating profitability from different customers, which helps the organization to decide on discounts to be extended to them, and which customers to focus more on.

This page is intentionally left blank

Chapter **5**

Support Department Cost Allocation

In this chapter, we shall see how the cost of support departments should be allocated.

The key learning objectives of this chapter are:

- Understand the need for correct allocation of costs of support departments

- Learn how to allocate costs of one support department

- Learn how to allocate costs of multiple support departments

Every company has two types of departments – operating departments and support departments. Operating departments are those that directly add value to the product or service provided by the company. Support departments provide services that assist other departments internal to the company.

5.1 Need for Cost Allocation

All direct costs are traced to the products or services. However, without allocating the support department costs or overheads, the costs could be misleading. The sections below show the decisions that could go wrong if support department costs are not correctly allocated.

Pricing Decisions

Companies use costs as the floor for pricing decisions. Any price above the cost brings profits to the company. If support department costs (indirect costs) are not allocated, it could result in a lower cost allocated to the company's products or services, thereby leading to incorrect pricing decisions.

Product/Department Profitability

Companies are always on the lookout to promote their more profitable products and services and improve upon or discontinue low profitable or loss-making products and services. Similarly, companies take decisions to grow or divest operating departments based on the profitability of those departments. Unless the indirect costs are properly allocated, it will not be possible to get a complete picture of the product, service, or department profitability.

5.2 Cost Allocation Basis

Support department costs are generally allocated using any one of the following criteria:

a) **Cause and effect** – When indirect costs are easy to allocate to operating departments based on their usage of the support departments resources, the cause and effect criteria is used. For example, the allocation of computer support department costs to operating departments can be based on their total usage of computer time.

b) **Benefits received** – indirect costs are allocated to operating departments based on the benefits they are expected to receive. For example, the costs of a marketing campaign could be allocated based on how much each operating department is expected to benefit from the promotion.

5.3 Allocating Costs of One Support Department

When there is just one support department in a company, its costs can be allocated to operating departments using two methods – Single-Rate method and Dual-Rate method. The difference between the two methods is the way they consider fixed and variable costs.

Single-Rate and Dual-Rate Methods

When the Single-Rate method is used to allocate support department costs, the costs are not converted into fixed and variable costs. Instead, a single total cost is used and directly allocated to the operating departments. The basis for allocating costs can be on the budgeted (or actual) usage, or total capacity. The following sections give an example of each of these methods.

For the Dual-Rate method, the support department costs are classified into fixed and variable costs and allocated separately. The basis for allocation is similar to the Single-Rate method.

Consider the example of a company that has one support department – the information technology department, and two operating departments – software services and hardware products. The support department provides computer services to the operating departments, and the capacity provided is based on the number of computer hours available. Below are the support department costs, budgeted hours of usage, and actual hours of usage by the operating departments:

Capacity of information technology department	20,000 hours
Fixed costs of information technology department	$50,000,000
Budgeted hours of usage of information technology department:	
Software services operating department	9,000 hours
Hardware products operating department	6,000 hours
Total	15,000 hours
Budgeted variable costs per hour	$100
Actual hours of usage of information technology department:	
Software services operating department	11,000 hours
Hardware products operating department	4,000 hours
Total	**15,000 hours**

Allocation based on Budgeted (or Actual) Usage

Using the Single-Rate method, the fixed and variable costs are added together to find the total cost of the support department. Then, the total cost per hour is calculated based on the budgeted hours. Finally, the total cost to be allocated to each operating department is calculated using the actual hours used. Shown below is the complete cost allocation using the Single-Rate method:

Budgeted Total cost ($50,000,000 + $100 x 15,000 hours) = $51,500,000

Budgeted rate per hour ($51,500,000/15,000 hours) = $3,433.33

Allocation to Software services department ($3,433.33 x 11,000 hours) = $37,766,666

Allocation to Hardware products department ($3,433.33 x 4,000 hours) = $13,733,333

Using the Dual-Rate method, the fixed cost per hour is computed using budgeted hours. The fixed and variable costs per hour are then used separately with the actual hours used to compute the total fixed and variable costs to be allocated to the operating departments separately. Budgeted hours are used with fixed costs, whereas, actual hours are used with variable costs. Shown below is the complete cost allocation using the Dual-Rate method:

Fixed cost per hour ($50,000,000/15,000 hours) = $3,333.33

Fixed costs allocated to Software services department ($3,333.33 x 9,000 hours) =$30,000,000

Variable costs allocated to Software services department ($100 x 11,000) = $1,100,000

Total costs allocated to Software services department = $31,100,000

Fixed costs allocated to Hardware products department ($3,333.33 x 6,000 hours) = $20,000,000

Variable costs allocated to Hardware products department ($100 x 4,000) = $400,000

Total costs allocated to Hardware products department = $20,400,000

As seen above, although the support department cost allocated to the two operating departments is quite different between the two methods, the total cost allocated is the same. This will always be the case as the support department cost incurred is the same, irrespective of the method used.

Allocation based on Total Capacity

This method uses the total capacity of the support department to allocate the fixed costs. This helps in unearthing how much capacity remains unutilized within the support department. It also does not consider some residual cost of the support department as the allocation of costs to the operating departments is not complete. This residual cost can be used by managers of that department to make a decision of reducing the capacity to save costs.

Once again, the Single-Rate method or the Dual-Rate method is used as shown below:

Fixed cost per hour ($50,000,000/20,000 hours) = $2,500

Variable cost per hour = $100

Using Single-Rate method

Budgeted rate per hour ($2,500 + $100) = $2,600

Allocation to Software services department ($2,600 x 11,000 hours) = $28,600,000

Allocation to Hardware products department ($2,600 x 4,000 hours) = $10,400,000

Unallocated ($2,600 x 5,000 hours) = $13,000,000

Using Dual-Rate method

Fixed costs allocated to the Software Services department ($2,500 x 9,000 hours) = $22,500,000

Variable costs allocated to the Software Services department ($100 x 11,000) = $1,100,000

Total costs allocated to the Software Services department = $23,600,000

Fixed costs allocated to Hardware Products department ($2,500 x 6,000 hours) = $15,000,000

Variable costs allocated to Hardware Products department ($100 x 4,000) = $400,000

Total costs allocated to Hardware Products department = $15,400,000

Unallocated ($2,600 x 5,000 hours) = $13,000,000

As seen above, there will be costs that remain unallocated. This data helps managers identify departments that have excess capacity that is not being used. They may use this data to take appropriate capacity reduction decisions to save costs.

5.4 Allocating Costs of Multiple Support Departments

When there are multiple support departments, cost allocation could be more complex as support departments may provide services to other support departments. There are three methods of allocation of support department costs when multiple support departments are present.

Direct Method

In this method, the costs of support departments are directly allocated to the operating departments. Even though the support departments provide services to each other, there is no cost allocation between them. Hence, this is a very simple method of cost allocation. Below is an example of a company with two support departments and two operating departments.

	Support Departments		Operating Departments		
	Mainte-nance	Computer Systems	Produc-tion	Packag-ing	Total
Budgeted overhead costs	$50,000	$100,000	$30,000	$40,000	$220,000
Support work done:					
By Maintenance					
Budgeted labor hours	-	2,800	7,000	4,200	14,000
Percentage	-	20%	50%	30%	100%
By Computer Systems					
Budgeted computer hours	500	-	2,000	2,500	5,000
Percentage	10%	-	40%	50%	100%

In the above data we see that both support departments provide services to each other as well. In Direct Method, we start allocating support department costs to the operating departments independent of this fact. Let's start with the Maintenance department. Its services are divided in the following ratio between the two operating departments based on the budgeted labor-hours:

Allocation to the Production department: 50%/(50% + 30%) = 5/8

Allocation to the Packaging department: 30%/(50% + 30%) = 3/8

Similarly, the computer systems services are divided as below based on the budgeted computer hours:

Allocation to the Production department: 40%/(40% + 50%) = 4/9

Allocation to the Packaging department: 50%/(40% + 50%) = 5/9

Below are the calculations:

	Support Departments		Operating Departments	
	Mainte-nance	Computer Systems	Produc-tion	Packag-ing
Budgeted overhead costs	$50,000	$100,000	$30,000	$40,000
Allocation of Maintenance costs (5/8, 3/8)	($50,000)	-	$31,250	$18,750
Allocation of Computer Systems costs (4/9, 5/9)	-	($100,000)	$44,444	$55,556
Total overhead of operating department	$0	$0	$105,694	$114,306

Below is a diagrammatic representation of the above cost allocation:

Figure 5.1

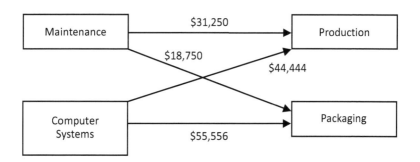

Step-Down Method

Using this method, support department costs are allocated to operating departments as well as other support departments. The sequence of allocation is therefore important. We start with the support department that provides more services to other support departments. In the above example, Maintenance provides 20% services to Computer Systems whereas Computer Systems provides only 10% services to Maintenance. Hence, we start with Maintenance first. Below are the allocation ratios for Maintenance:

Allocation to the Computer Systems department: 20%/(20% + 50% + 30%) = 2/10

Allocation to the Production department: 50%/(20% + 50% + 30%) = 5/10

Allocation to the Packaging department: 30%/(20% + 50% + 30%) = 3/10

Allocation of the Computer Systems department happens using the same ratio as above as there is no further allocation from Computer Systems to Maintenance. Below are the calculations:

	Support Departments		Operating Departments	
	Mainte-nance	Computer Systems	Produc-tion	Packag-ing
Budgeted overhead costs	$50,000	$100,000	$30,000	$40,000
Allocation of Maintenance costs (2/10, 5/10, 3/10)	($50,000)	$10,000	$25,000	$15,000
		$110,000		
Allocation of Computer Systems costs (4/9, 5/9)	-	($110,000)	$48,889	$61,111
Total overhead of operating departments	$0	$0	$103,889	$116,111

Below is a diagrammatic representation of the above cost allocation:

Figure 5.2

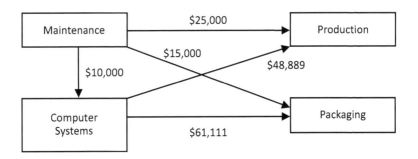

Reciprocal Method

In this method, the support departments allocate costs to other support departments and operating departments over and over again, until all costs have been allocated. So in the above case, the Maintenance department would allocate costs to the Computer Systems, Production and Packaging departments. Then the Computer Systems departments would allocate costs to Maintenance, Production and Packaging and so on, until all support department costs have been completely allocated. In order to simplify this long procedure, mathematical equations are used based on allocation between the support departments. For the above example, the following two equations would be used:

$M = \$50,000 + 0.1CS$

$CS = \$100,000 + 0.2M$

Where, M stands for Maintenance department costs and CS stands for the costs of Computer Systems department.

Solving the two equations gives:

M = $50,000 + 0.1 x ($100,000 + 0.2M) = $50,000 + $10,000 + 0.02M = $60,000 + 0.02M

Therefore, M = $60,000/0.98 = $61,224.5

And CS = $100,000 + 0.2 x $61,224.5 = $112,244.9

These values are then used to allocate to the operating departments as below:

	Support Departments		Operating Departments	
	Mainte-nance	Computer Systems	Produc-tion	Packag-ing
Budgeted overhead costs	$50,000	$100,000	$30,000	$40,000
Allocation of Maintenance costs (2/10, 5/10, 3/10)	($61,225)	$12,245	$30,612	$18,367
Allocation of Computer Systems costs (1/10, 4/10, 5/10)	$11,224	($112,245)	$44,898	$56,122
Total overhead of operating departments	($0)	$0	$105,510	$114,490

The only difference between this method and the Step-Down method is that the allocation of support department costs is not done using the overhead of that department. Instead, an amount is computed using the equations first, based on the inter-department allocation, and that amount is used for allocating the costs of one support department at a time.

Below is a diagrammatic representation of the above cost allocation:

Figure 5.3

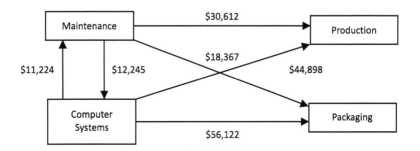

Solved Examples

1. AAA Inc. has four operating departments (A, B, C, and D) and one support department, P. The manufacturing departments take power from the support department based on the following capacity and expected usage:

Operating Department	Required Capacity of P (in KWh)	Expected Usage of P (in KWh)
A	10,000	8,000
B	20,000	9,000
C	12,000	7,000
D	8,000	6,000
Total	50,000	30,000

The total cost of department P is $1,500,000, out of which $600,000 is variable and $900,000 is fixed.

a. Compute the allocation of support department costs to the operating departments using the Single-Rate method, based on the required capacity.

b. Use the Dual-Rate method to allocate the support department costs. Allocate fixed cost based on the required capacity and variable cost based on the expected usage.

Solution:

a. Single-Rate method has only one cost pool as below:

Total cost = $1,500,000

Total required capacity = 50,000 KWh

Cost per KWh = $1,500,000/50,000 = $30 per KWh

Below are the cost allocations:

	A	B	C	D
Required Capacity	10,000	20,000	12,000	8,000
Cost allocated (@$30/KWh)	$300,000.00	$ 600,000.00	$ 360,000.00	$ 240,000.00

b. Dual-Rate method differentiates between fixed and variable costs. We are required to consider the required capacity for allocating fixed costs and the expected usage for allocating variable costs. Below are the cost pools:

Fixed cost = $900,000

Total required capacity = 50,000 KWh

Fixed cost per KWh = $900,000/$50,000 = $18 per KWh

Variable cost = $600,000

Total expected usage = 30,000 KWh

Variable cost per KWh = $600,000/30,000 = $20 per KWh

Below are the cost allocations:

	A	B	C	D
Required Capacity	10,000	20,000	12,000	8,000
Fixed Cost allocated (@$18/KWh)	$180,000.00	$360,000.00	$216,000.00	$144,000.00
Expected Usage	8,000	9,000	7,000	6,000
Variable Cost allocated (@20/KWh)	$160,000.00	$180,000.00	$140,000.00	$120,000.00
Total Cost allocated	340,000.00	540,000.00	356,000.00	264,000.00

2. **XYZ Inc. has two operating departments and two support departments. Below is the data related to costs and other relevant details of these departments:**

Department	Revenue	Cost	No. of employees	Pages printed
Wholesale Sales	$1,334,200	$998,270	42	1,920
Retail Sales	$667,100	$489,860	28	1,600
HR	-	$72,700	14	320
Printing	-	$234,400	21	1,120

Use the number of employees to allocate the costs of the HR department and the number of pages printed to allocate the costs of the Printing department.

a. **Allocate the support department costs using the Direct method.**

b. **Use the Reciprocal method to perform the cost allocation.**

Solution:

a. In the Direct method, the costs of the two support departments are allocated to the operating departments without any allocation made to each other.

Let's start with the HR department. Its services are divided into the following ratio between the two operating departments based on budgeted labor-hours:

Allocation to the Wholesale Sales department: $42/(42 + 28) = 0.6$

Allocation to the Retail Sales department: $28/(42 + 28) = 0.4$

Similarly, the Printing department costs are divided as follows based on pages printed:

Allocation to the Wholesale Sales department: 1,920/(1,920 + 1,600) = 0.545

Allocation to the Retail Sales department: 1,600/(1,920 + 1,600)

= 0.455

Below are the calculations:

	Support Departments		Operating Departments	
	HR	Printing	Wholesale sales	Retail sales
Budgeted overhead costs	$72,700	$234,400	$998,270	$489,860
Allocation of HR costs (0.6, 0.4))	($72,700)	-	$43,620	$29,080
Allocation of Printing costs (0.545, 0.455)	-	($234,400)	$127,748	$106,652
Total overhead of operating departments	$0	$0	$1,169,638	$625,592

b. To use the Reciprocal method, we need to solve two equations representing the allocation of support department costs on each other as shown below:

HR = $72,700 + (320/(1,920 + 1,600 + 320)) x P = $72,700 + 0.08333P

P = $234,400 + (21/(42 + 28 + 21)) x HR = $234,400 + 0.23077HR

Solving the above equations:

HR = $72,700 + 0.08333 x ($234,400 + 0.23077HR) = $72,700 + $19,532.55 + 0.01923HR

Hence, HR = $92,232.55/0.98077 = $94,041

And P = $234,400 + 0.23077 x $94,041 = $256,102

Shown below are the cost allocations using this method:

	Support Departments		Operating Departments	
	HR	Printing	Wholesale sales	Retail sales
Budgeted overhead costs	$72,700	$234,400	$998,270	$489,860
Allocation of HR costs (21/91, 42/91, 28/91)	($94,041)	$21,702	$43,404	$28,936
Allocation of Printing costs (320/3,840, 1,920/3,840,1,600/3,840)	$21,342	($256,102)	$128,051	$106,709
Total overhead of operating departments	$1	($0)	$1,169,725	$625,505

There is some residual value left in the support departments due to a rounding-off error.

Practice Exercise

1. Describe the differences between support and operating departments. Give two examples for each.

2. ZZZ Inc. prices its products at a full cost plus 30% of the full cost. The company operates two support departments and two operating departments. Budgeted costs and normal activity levels are as follows:

	Support Departments		Operating Departments	
	W	X	Y	Z
Overhead costs	$40,000	$100,000	$180,000	$240,000
Square feet	1,000	1,200	2,000	6,000
No of employees	20	30	60	40
Labor hours	-	-	10,000	6,400
Machine hours	-	-	6,000	10,800

Support department W's costs are allocated based on the square feet parameter and support department X's costs are allocated based on the number of employees.

a. Use the Direct method of cost allocation to find the overheads allocated to each operating department.

Department Y uses labor hours to assign overhead costs to products, while department Z uses machine hours. One of the products the company produces requires 4 labor hours per unit in department Y, and no time at all in department Z. Direct materials for the product cost $180 per unit and direct labor is $80 per unit. Compute the selling price of the company's products based on the above pricing policy.

Solutions to the above questions can be downloaded from the **Online Resources** *section of this book on* **www.vibrantpublishers.com**

Chapter Summary

◆ Without allocating the support department or overhead costs, the costing of products is incomplete. Incomplete allocation of support department costs provides us with incorrect data for making pricing decisions for the company's products. Hence, the calculation of the profitability of products and of the company's different departments will also be incorrect.

◆ When allocating costs of one support department, we can use the single-rate method or the dual-rate method. The single-rate method does not separate fixed and variable costs while the dual-rate method considers them separately. Cost allocation can happen based on budgeted or actual usage or based on capacity. When it is based on capacity, some unallocated costs of the support department could remain. This helps managers of that department to cut the excess capacity.

◆ When allocating costs of multiple support departments, we use the direct method, where the support department costs are allocated only to the operating departments. When using the step-down method, support department costs are allocated to operating departments as well as the other support departments. In the Reciprocal method, support department costs are allocated to the operating departments and other support departments over and over again until all costs have been allocated.

Chapter **6**

Cost Control

In this chapter, we shall look at how cost control is done.

The key learning objectives of this chapter are:

- Understand the different types of cost variances

- Learn how to calculate the different types of cost variances

Every company creates a budget that serves as a baseline for their business. They also compare the actual performance with the budgeted planned performance and calculate the variances. A variance is any deviation from the budget.

Companies create mainly three kinds of budgets. The first one is for revenue; the second is for the Direct costs and the third is for the Indirect costs. Variances against each of these are calculated differently. The sections below show which variances are calculated and how to interpret them.

6.1 Direct Variances

There are two kinds of direct variances – revenue and cost.

Revenue Variance

All companies create a budget of how much amount of a particular product or service they would sell in the year and at what price. This is shown as:

$$Budgeted\ Revenue = Price \times Quantity$$

If there is a deviation in the revenue, it leads to a Revenue Variance as shown below:

$$Total\ Revenue\ Variance = Actual\ Revenue - Budgeted\ Revenue$$

This variance could occur due to a smaller or larger quantity sold and/or lower or higher price of each unit. Hence, the above total revenue variance can actually be broken down into two parts as shown below:

$$Total\ Revenue\ Variance = Revenue\ Quantity\ Variance + Revenue\ Price\ Variance$$

The revenue quantity variance is due to the difference between the budgeted and actual quantities. The revenue price variance is due to the difference between the budgeted and actual prices. The two variances are:

$$Revenue\ Quantity\ Variance = (AQ - SQ) \times SP$$

$$Revenue\ Price\ Variance = (AP - SP) \times AQ$$

Where,

AQ is the Actual quantity

SQ is the Standard (or budgeted) quantity

AP is the Actual price

SP is the Standard (or budgeted) price

Hence, the Total Revenue Variance = (AQ – SQ) x SP + (AP – SP) x AQ

= AQ x SP – SQ x SP + AP x AQ – SP x AQ = AP x AQ – SQ x SP = Actual revenue – Budgeted revenue

In the above equation, SQ x SP stands for Standard (or budgeted) revenue and AP x AQ stands for Actual revenue. It may also be noted that while calculating quantity variance, we use the standard price and with price variance, we use the actual quantity. This is the most frequently used way of computing variances, but it can also be done in another way.

Let's take an example. Consider a company that sells only one product. It has created the following revenue budget:

Table 6.1

	Standard (or budgeted)	Actual
Quantity	1,000 (SQ)	950 (AQ)
Price	$40 (SP)	$50 (AP)

Total Revenue Variance = (950 x $50) – (1,000 x $40) = $47,500 – $40,000 = $7,500 (F)

As seen above, the total revenue variance is favorable by $7,500. This is because the company has managed to earn revenue that is more than it budgeted for. However, the complete story is not yet known unless the individual variances are also calculated. These calculations are shown below:

Revenue Quantity Variance = $(950 - 1{,}000) \times \$40 = -\$2{,}000$ (U)

Revenue Price Variance = $(\$50 - \$40) \times 950 = \$9{,}500$ (F)

The individual variances reveal that the company sold a lesser quantity (an unfavorable variance) at a higher price (a favorable variance). This may mean that the sales team decided to increase the selling price of the product at the expense of losing some sales. But it had, overall, resulted in a favorable outcome for the company's revenues.

Direct Cost Variance

Every product or service has two types of costs – direct and indirect costs. The direct costs are generally direct labor and direct material costs. Any variance in the budgeted quantity of materials used, labor used, or their rates can give a direct cost variance. These variances are very similar to the revenue variance seen earlier. The Total Direct Cost Variance is:

Total Direct Cost Variance = Actual Direct Costs – Standard (or budgeted) Direct Costs

This variance can be caused due to these factors:

a) Quantity of direct materials used (using a lesser or greater quantity of raw materials)

b) Price of direct materials used (buying raw materials at a lower or higher price)

c) Quantity of direct labor used (using a smaller or larger quantity of labor)

d) Price of direct labor used (hiring labor at a lower or higher price)

Accordingly, the total direct cost variance can be split into four components. Let's first look at each of these components individually.

When a company uses a raw material for lesser than it budgeted for, it will save money – it will have a favorable Material Usage Variance as shown below.

$$Material\ Usage\ Variance = (SQ - AQ) \times SP$$

Where, SQ, AQ, and SP are all standard and actual values for direct materials used

Similarly, when the company uses more labor than it initially budgeted for, it will spend more money – it will have an unfavorable Labor Efficiency Variance as shown.

$$Labor\ Efficiency\ Variance = (SQ - AQ) \times SP\ (Note:\ this\ is\ similar\ to\ material\ usage\ variance)$$

Where, SQ, AQ, and SP are all standard and actual values for direct labor used

In the same way, there can be two price variances due to the differences between the budgeted and actual price of the raw materials or labor.

$$Purchase\ Price\ Variance = (SP - AP) \times AQ$$

Where, SP, AP, and AQ are all standard and actual values for direct materials used

$$Labor\ Rate\ Variance = (SP - AP) \times AQ$$

(Note: this is similar to the purchase price variance)

Where, SP, AP, and AQ are all standard and actual values for direct labor used

The total variance is then given as:

Total Direct Cost Variance = Material Usage Variance + Labor Efficiency Variance + Purchase Price Variance + Labor Rate Variance

Let's take an example to illustrate the Direct cost variances. Assume a company produces woolen jackets. The only raw material used is wool. From the past data, the company creates a direct cost budget for the next year as shown below (this is to make one jacket):

Table 6.2

	Quantity	Price	Standard (or budgeted)
Wool	5 yarns (SQ - materials)	$2 (SP - materials)	$10
Labor	3 hours (SQ - labor)	$10 (SP - labor)	$30
Total			$40

At the end of the year the company gathers the actual values as below:

Table 6.3

	Quantity	Price	Actual
Wool	4.5 yarns (AQ – materials)	$2.25 (AP – materials)	$10.125
Labor	2 hours (AQ – labor)	$12 (AP – labor)	$24
Total			$34.125

If the company simply calculates the total direct cost variance then it gets:

Total Direct Cost Variance = $40 - $34.125 = $5.875 (F)

Although the company has a favorable variance, this is not the end of the story, as the company still does not know which departments performed well. In order to know this, it needs to compute the individual direct material and direct labor variances.

Material Usage Variance = (5 – 4.5) x $2 = $1 (F)

Labor Efficiency Variance = (3 – 2) x $10 = $10 (F)

Purchase Price Variance = ($2 - $2.25) x 4.5 = -$1.125 (U)

Labor Rate Variance = ($10 - $12) x 2 = -$4 (U)

Now we can clearly understand which department of the company has performed well and which has not, and how much each department contributed to the favorable total variance. From the above example, it seems like the company did well in reducing the use of raw materials, which could be due to a reduction in waste. The company also took lesser time, showing an increase in employee productivity. However, the company spent more money on buying raw materials and also in hiring labor – possibly due to temporary labor or multiple shifts that work out costlier. The individual variance information helps the company analyze areas of concern so as to take corrective action.

6.2 Indirect Variances

Most companies have Indirect costs. They are all the overhead costs like rent, depreciation, power, etc. Variances of these costs are more difficult to compute as they cannot be easily traced to the product or service. There are two ways to compute variances of such costs.

Fixed Budgeting

In this approach, all the overhead (or indirect) costs are budgeted using the expected sales volume. No matter how much the actual sales are, the variances are calculated using this fixed budget only.

For example, consider the following budgeted overhead costs:

Table 6.4

Item	Budgeted Cost	Type of Cost
Rent	$10,000	Fixed
Depreciation	$20,000	Fixed
Power	$5,000	Semi-variable
Office supplies	$500	Semi-variable
Plant supervision	$1,000	Step cost
Total	$36,500	

Some of the above costs are purely fixed, whereas, others are semi-variable. Rent and depreciation are fixed overheads that do not vary with the production volume. However, power, office supplies, and plant supervision may vary with production volume – they are either semi-variable or a step cost. A step cost is one that is fixed over a certain relevant range, beyond which it changes in a lump. Plant supervision is one such cost. Until, for example, 120% of the expected production, the plant may function with a single supervisor. But if the production goes beyond that, another supervisor needs to be hired until the production goes beyond 200%.

In the above example, the overheads are budgeted for a normal production volume of 100,000 units. Now, if the number of units produced in the year is 150,000, then the semi-variable costs – power and office supplies – will go up. This may make the company believe that they have spent more on power than budgeted and that the variance is unfavorable. But in reality, it is only because of more production. Similar cases can happen with plant supervision, which is a step cost. Hence, this method would lead to incorrect conclusions. This happens because this method treats all overheads as fixed costs.

Flexible Budgeting

This method gives due credit to the overhead costs that are not fixed. Instead of having a single fixed budget for overheads, the company prepares several budgets based on varying levels of production:

Table 6.5

Capacity Utilization ->	60%	70%	80%	100%
Units Produced ->	60,000	70,000	80,000	100,000
Rent	$10,000	$10,000	$10,000	$10,000
Depreciation	$20,000	$20,000	$20,000	$20,000
Power	$4,000	$4,200	$4,500	$5,000
Office supplies	$425	$450	$475	$500
Plant supervision	$500	$1,000	$1,000	$1,500
Total	$34,925	$35,650	$35,975	$37,000

Now, depending upon the capacity utilization for the year, the appropriate flexible budget is used to compute the variances. This gives a much more realistic picture of variances. The Total Overhead at each level of production is called the Allowed Overhead. The overhead the company actually incurs at budgeted capacity (assume 100% in this case) is called the Actual Overhead. Finally, the overhead cost included or absorbed in the products is called the Absorbed Overhead. Below are examples using the above data:

At 60% capacity utilization

Allowed Overhead = $34,925

Actual Overhead = $37,000

Absorbed Overhead - Computed based on how much has been included in each product that is sold. For example, if 1,000 units of a product are sold and each unit includes an Indirect cost of $35, then the absorbed overhead is $35,000.

At 70% capacity utilization

Allowed Overhead = $35,650

Actual Overhead = $37,000

At 80% capacity utilization

Allowed Overhead = $35,975

Actual Overhead = $37,000

At 100% capacity utilization

Allowed Overhead = $37,000

Actual Overhead = $37,000

Total Variance = Actual Overhead – Absorbed Overhead

It has these two components:

Volume Variance = Allowed Overhead – Absorbed Overhead

Spending Variance = Actual Overhead – Allowed Overhead

Hence,

Total Variance = Volume Variance + Spending Variance

Solved Examples

1. AAA Inc. has budgeted the direct materials, direct manufacturing labor and direct distribution cost per consignment as $100, $50 and $70 respectively. The actual performance is shown below:

	Actual Costs
Direct Materials	$900,000
Direct manufacturing labor	$450,000
Direct distribution	$500,000

The above actual costs are computed with reference to an actual output of 8,000 units of the product as against the budgeted output of 10,000 units.

a. Compute the Direct variances for the company.

b. Comment on the variances.

Solution:

a. The actual costs are incurred for 8,000 units. We can compute the per-unit cost of each cost item (direct materials, direct manufacturing labor, direct distribution) as shown:

	Total Costs	Per Unit Cost
Direct Materials	$900,000.00	$112.50
Direct manufacturing labor	$450,000.00	$56.25
Direct distribution	$500,000.00	$62.50

The above per-unit costs are compared with the budgeted costs below along with the individual variances:

	Actual	Budgeted	Variance	Type
Direct Materials	$112.50	$100.00	($12.50)	Unfavorable
Direct manufacturing labor	$56.25	$50.00	($6.25)	Unfavorable
Direct distribution	$62.50	$70.00	$7.50	Favorable
Total	$231.25	$220.00	($11.25)	Unfavorable

b. There are unfavorable variances for direct materials and direct manufacturing labor. This means that the company has spent more than the budgeted amount on these two direct cost items. The direct distribution variance is favorable, pointing towards a spend that is lower than the budgeted value.

2. XYZ Inc. buys internet access time from other companies in bulk to sell to its retail customers. It budgets to buy 80,000 minutes at $0.05 per minute. However, the actual purchases through the year are 100,000 minutes at $0.065 per minute due to increased demand. The company also budgets a pay of $15 per hour to workers for the installation of services. The installation effort is budgeted to be 1 hour for 500 minutes of internet access time. The actual rate it pays to workers is $14.50 and it pays for a total of 180 hours.

   a. Compute direct material variances.

   b. Compute direct labor variances.

   c. Compute total direct cost variance.

Solution:

   a. Direct material budgets and actual budgets are directly given and the variances are calculated as shown below:

   Material usage variance = (SQ – AQ) x SP = (80,000 – 100,000) x $0.05 = -$1,000 (U)

   Purchase Price variance = (SP – AP) x AQ = ($0.05 - $0.065) x 100,000 = -$1,500 (U)

   b. Direct labor variances are calculated like this:

   Labor efficiency variance = (SQ – AQ) x SP

   SQ = 1 hour x (80,000/500 minutes) = 160 hours

   AQ = 180 hours

   Therefore, Labor efficiency variance = (160 – 180) x $15 = -$300 (U)

Labor rate variance =(SP – AP) x AQ = ($15 - $14.50) x 180 = $90 (F)

c. Total direct cost variance = (-$1,000) + (-$1,500) + (-$300) + $90 = -$2,710

3. **ZZZ Inc. manufactures a monthly normal production of 10,000 units of a product. The standard factory overhead rates are based on a normal monthly volume of one standard hour per unit. The standard factory rates per direct labor hours are:**

Fixed	$6.00
Variable	$10.00

Units actually produced in the current month are 9,000. Actual factory overhead costs incurred (includes $70,000 fixed) are $156,000. Actual direct labor hours are 9,000.

What is the variable overhead spending variance for the company?

Solution:

Variable overhead spending variance = Actual variable overhead – Allowed variable overhead

Actual variable overhead = $156,000 - $70,000 = $86,000

Allowed variable overhead = 9,000 x $10 = 90,000

Therefore,

Variable overhead spending variance = $86,000 - $90,000 = -$4,000 (F)

The above variance is favorable since the actual variable overhead is lower than allowed. This means that the company has spent less than it was allowed to spend on the variable overheads at 9,000 units of production.

Practice Exercise

1. AAA Inc. manufactures 100-pound bags of fertilizers that
   have the following unit standard costs for direct materials
   and direct labor:

Direct materials (100 lbs @ $1.00 per lb)	$100.00
Direct labor (0.5 hours @ $24 per hour)	$12.00
Total standard direct cost per 100 lb bag	$112.00

   The following activities were recorded for the month:

   1,000 bags were manufactured

   95,000 lbs. of materials costing $76,000 were purchased

   102,500 lbs. of materials were used

   $12,000 was paid for 475 hours of direct labor

   There was no beginning or ending work-in-process
   inventories.

   a. Compute direct material variances.

   b. Compute direct labor variances.

   c. Give possible reasons for the occurrence of each of the
      preceding variances.

2. XYZ Inc. makes chocolates. For the month it budgeted to purchase and use 15,000 lb of cocoa at $17.80. The actual purchase and usage was 16,000 lb at $16.40. It had budgeted for 3,750 lb of chocolates. The actual output was 3,800 lb of chocolates.

    a. Compute direct material variances.

    b. Comment on the performance of the company.

3. ZZZ Inc. has a capacity of 5,000 units. The standard factory overhead rate is based on a normal monthly volume of 0.5 standard hour per unit. The standard factory variable rate per hour is $50. The units actually produced in the current month are 4,500. The actual factory variable overhead costs incurred are $100,000. The actual direct labor hours are 2,250.

What is the variable overhead spending variance for the company?

Solutions to the above questions can be downloaded from the **Online Resources** *section of this book on* **www.vibrantpublishers.com**

Chapter Summary

◆ Variances are a deviation from the budget. They are calculated for revenue, direct costs, and variable costs.

◆ Revenue variance can occur due to differences in quantity (revenue quantity variance) or differences in price (revenue price variance).

◆ Direct costs variance could be due to differences in the quantity of material used (material usage variance), the productivity of labor (labor efficiency variance), the purchase price of materials (purchase price variance), or manpower cost (labor rate variance).

◆ Indirect costs variance uses either the fixed budgeting method or the flexible budgeting method. The fixed budgeting method could give erroneous results, as it treats all overheads as fixed costs. The flexible budgeting method differentiates the indirect costs variance based on a change in volume (volume variance) and change in costs (spending variance). It gives a more correct picture of the indirect costs variance

This page is intentionally left blank

Chapter 7

Customer Profitability

This chapter introduces customer relationship management (CRM) and customer profitability analysis as critical financial functions of an organization. The financial viability of a business depends on its revenues, and ultimately its customers or clients (collectively referred to as customers for the rest of this chapter for the sake of brevity). At the end of the day, all the financial planning in the world is of very little value if there is no revenue. Customers are the lifeblood of the business. Therefore, it is vital an organization understands the needs of its customers as well as their profitability. Companies will sometimes make the mistake of focusing on just product profitability and not realizing this is, at best, a very incomplete picture of the business. This chapter will also discuss the information systems necessary to maximize the understanding of this important concept.

Key learning objectives include the reader's understanding of the following:

- The importance of customer profitability
- Ways to increase revenue and profitability

- Customer Relationship Management (CRM) systems

- The difference between customer and product profitability analysis

- How activitybased costing (ABC) and cost drivers work

- Action steps for unprofitable products and customers

7.1 Why Is Understanding Customer Profitability So Important?

Increasing revenue is a typical goal of most business organizations. There are only a few ways through which a business can increase revenue:

- Sell more of the same product to the current customers;

- Sell additional products to the current customers (cross-selling);

- Sell a more profitable mix of the products (i.e. products with higher gross profit) to the current customers (upselling); and

- Find and sell to new customers.

Of these, finding new customers is probably the most difficult. It costs valuable time and money to generate new customers. Think of the advertising and sales activity it takes to identify, contact, and attract new customers. Therefore, customer retention should be a top priority of every business. To remain competitive and grow the business, it is imperative to keep customers longer and hopefully grow them into larger customers. A business should strive to serve each customer more efficiently and make them more profitable.

In today's business climate many products are perceived as being commodities, with the competition between companies occurring more and more in product differentiation and service. Many times, this information and the accompanying costs are not captured in the product profitability system. Examples of this are warehousing and interest expenses. The situation is complicated further, as technology now allows for market segmentation and individualized marketing programs. All of this costs money and requires business intelligence.

7.2 Customer Information Systems

Technology makes business information systems more and more accessible to even the smallest companies today. Besides having a general ledger (accounting) system, more and more organizations can afford an Enterprise Resource Planning (ERP) system and a Customer Relationship Management (CRM) system. The typical ERP system assists in production and inventory planning, while a CRM provides critical information about customers. The ERP system should provide at least rudimentary product profitability data.

Even a modest CRM system will track the entire "customer journey" from sales calls to orders to sales to accounts receivables. It will also provide places to record such information like conversations with customers, notes made by the sales personnel, credit limits, and scheduled customer contacts. The goal of a

CRM is to efficiently manage the customer relationship from the company's perspective and to provide excellent service from the customer's point of view. Having this information available from the CRM increases the possibility of upselling and cross-selling to a customer, which are two ways to increase revenue.

7.3 From Product to Customer Profitability

The cost accounting system only captures and analyzes data dealing with the sale of inventory, called the cost of goods sold by accountants. However, this is only one type of cost incurred when dealing with a customer. A more complete financial information system will include these other costs when determining customer profitability. They are directly related to customer profitability but are not included in the cost of goods sold. Consequently, moving from just understanding product profitability to understanding customer profitability should be the goal of every business organization.

Figure 7.1

With this background, let's look at a simple example of a customer profitability analysis.

Suppose your company sells inventory with a cost of $500 to Customer A for $1,000. The gross profit on the sale is $500 ($1,000 sales price less the inventory cost of $500), resulting in a gross profit percentage of 50%! Surely this must be a profitable customer. Upon closer inspection though, Customer A's profitability is not nearly as big as you might think. Let's look at the selling expenses associated with the sale. The salesmen will receive a 7% commission for the sale. If the terms of the shipment are FOB (free on board) Destination, the seller will need to pay the freight. It is not uncommon for shipping expenses to be 15% of revenue in the United States. "Freight out" is considered a selling expense for financial accounting purposes and will also not be captured in the cost accounting system. Suppose the customer is difficult, and often "charges back" (takes discounts) of 5% of total sales for various contractual violations such as quality and shipment issues. Just these three additional costs total 27% of the sales to Customer A. The profit on the transaction has now been reduced to $230, or 23% of sales revenue.

This is still a fairly healthy profit margin but that is not all of the costs we need to consider. If the general and administrative expenses of the company are an additional 10% of sales and interest expense is 5% of sales (generally considered a good number for a well-run company) the pre-tax income is now just $80. Suppose the company has an effective tax rate of 25%. The final profit on the sale is $60, or only six percent of total sales. What started out as a promising, extremely profitable sale to Customer A resulted in a rather ordinary return on sales (ROS) of 6% to the owners.

Having a customer profitability system that takes into account the additional costs beyond the inventory costs gives management a more accurate picture of the customer relationship than simply looking at product profitability information. Having this information allows management to formulate a plan to increase Customer A's profitability and maintain a high level of service. There are several levers management can lean on immediately to try to increase the profitability of Company A sales. For example, why is Company A taking chargebacks? The management could ask questions such as: Are there quality control issues with the product sold to Customer A? Could there be a problem with shipments? Secondly, the management could try to negotiate better terms for the freight costs, increasing profitability.

There are also some longer-term solutions as well. Your company should attempt to move the performance evaluation measures from sales to profitability on sales, wherever possible. For example, higher commissions could be paid on higher profit items. Attempts can be made to cross-sell and upsell to Customer A. Achievement of these goals will be recorded and monitored in the CRM.

7.4 Activity-Based Costing

The astute reader will note our customer profitability model is not quite correct at this point since it still relies on the allocation of some general and administrative expenses. Allocating expenses is often inaccurate, since this does not relate the actual expense of each supporting activity to the actual customer.

As an example of this premise, let's take a look at a sales administrative function. A company may have staff members devoted to dealing with such issues as routine customer questions, processing orders, and coordinating shipment details with the customer. The expense of maintaining such a department will often be considered an indirect expense and allocated to customers, most likely on the basis of sales dollars. This can be inaccurate though, as a customer who places one large order rather than making many smaller orders would ordinarily require less handling and intervention by the sales administration department and therefore should be regarded as a more profitable customer.

One way to more effectively determine customer product profitability is through the use of **activity-based costing** (ABC). ABC uses **cost drivers** to trace costs to cost objects, based on their utilization. The goal is to trace as many costs as possible rather than allocating them. Companies should try to use fewer and fewer allocations in decision-making, since an allocated expense may not be entirely relevant to product pricing considerations.

Suppose if in our previous example, the other selling, general, and administrative expenses were allocated on the basis of total sales dollars for each customer. In the case of the sales administration department, the number of sales orders processed could be a good way to measure the utilization of the department and could be considered the cost driver. If Customer A accounts for 10% of the total orders processed by the sales administration department, it will be charged that percentage of the department's annual budget. Note that this could yield a drastically different customer profitability calculation if Customer A accounts for only 5% of total sales. Moving to ABC accounting will double the sales administration expense Customer A will absorb.

Cost drivers can be used throughout the organization to trace rather than allocate costs. The following table contains just a few examples of how costs can be traced rather than allocated.

Table 7.1

Function	Potential Cost Drivers
Collection department	Past due receivables during the year
Plant maintenance department	Hours spent cleaning after the manufacture of certain products
Purchasing department	Number of orders for raw materials
Training department	Number of employees

Of course, setting up an activity-based costing system is not as easy as it sounds, and a company may need to get outside assistance in doing this. ABC has a reputation for being difficult to implement and requiring tedious amounts of record keeping. However, the management can implement ABC over a period of years, developing the cost driver system over that time period. A smaller organization may be able to capture and portray a substantial amount of its operating costs with as less as thirty cost drivers. The value of doing all of this work is getting additional information about each customer's profitability and therefore better decisions about how to manage customer accounts.

7.5 Unprofitable Customers and Products

The *Pareto Principle* (also known as the 80-20 rules) states 80% of customer profitability will come from 20% of the customers. While this is not a hard and fast rule, it does demonstrate why it is necessary to study each customer's profitability. Let's suppose that after the financial manager is done analyzing the data, a product has been found to be unprofitable. Should it be discontinued? All other things being equal, the answer is yes. However, there are many exceptions to this rule. First of all, a product can be a *loss leader*, a product sold at a loss in order to entice customers to shop for other products. One notorious example of using this strategy is Walmart, who for years would sell toys during the Christmas season at less than their cost. Walmart simply wanted to give shoppers an incentive to visit their stores during the Christmas season. In effect, the loss in sales of toys was really a type of advertising. This strategy was one of the main reasons why Toy R'us, a major toy retailer, was forced into bankruptcy. It could not survive by selling its products below the cost. Another example of the loss leader product is the way pharmacy stores operate. Traditionally, the pharmacy counter does not contribute very much to store profits. However, it is located at the back of the store and customers must walk through the store to reach the pharmacy counter. They have an opportunity to shop and buy profits with a much higher profit margin.

Secondly, each product has its own *life cycle*. Products are introduced, sales increase, flatten out and decline over time when they are pushed out by newer products. In the early phases of its life cycle, a product may be unprofitable. However, if the expectation is that the product will eventually become profitable then it should not be abandoned. A third reason not to abandon an unprofitable product is *unused or excess plant capacity*. While the sale of the product may not be profitable under full absorption costing (including direct material, direct labor, and overhead costs), it may still help defray fixed costs that are part of overhead costs.

Unprofitable customers also present unique challenges. As was mentioned earlier, finding new customers is extremely difficult and costly. Jettisoning a customer should be a last resort. The management needs to review such customers on a regular basis to see if there are immediate actions that can be taken to improve customer profitability. Failing that, the management will then need to see if there are actions that can improve future profitability. For instance, can prices be raised or can sales terms be changed to reduce outstanding credit? Finally, the management will need to project if the sales to this customer will increase and/or the sales mix will become more profitable. Only after such an exhaustive review should such a customer be turned away.

Solved Examples

1. The customer profitability system reports the following for Customer B:

Total sales	$1,000,000
Cost of goods sold	400,000
Product advertising	100,000

Sales commissions are 5% of total sales. Customer B will "chargeback" (take discounts of 3%) of sales. Customer B also demands the Company keep $100,000 of safety stock inventory available at all times. The annual carrying cost of inventory is 10%. Customer B takes shipment of its inventory four times of even amounts throughout the year. How profitable is Customer B?

Solution:

The gross profit on the sales is $600,000 (Sales of $1 million less the cost of goods sold of $400,000). Your company has contractually agreed to provide $100,000 in advertising to support the sales of the product by Customer B. Additional deductions are the sales commission expense of $50,000 and the discounts taken (chargebacks) by Customer B of $30,000. The most difficult part of the computation is the inventory carrying costs. Since the cost of goods sold for the year is $400,000 and Customer B takes four shipments during the year, your company will need to have $100,000 of inventory available for each shipment date. Assuming this inventory is being built evenly throughout the quarter, the average inventory on hand for the next shipment will be $50,000 plus the safety stock of

$100,000 the customer requires you to have. Therefore, on average the carrying cost of Customer B's inventory is $15,000 (The average inventory of $150,000 times 10%). Therefore, the business relationship with Customer B will produce a profit of $405,000 for the year (Gross profit of $600,000 less advertising of $100,000; sales commissions of $50,000; sales discounts of $30,000 and inventory carrying costs of $15,000.) Therefore, even though the customer takes sales discounts the relationship appears to be a highly profitable one.

Nevertheless, one cannot be too complacent in this situation. Taxes, which are not considered in this example, can reduce overall profit and consequently cash flow considerably. Additionally, studies have shown inventory carrying costs can be as high as 30% in the current business climate, further reducing profitability.

2. **If you were responsible for the financial management of your company, how would you review Customer B?**

Solution:

While Customer B is certainly profitable, there are several factors requiring immediate attention. First, why does Customer B require such a large safety stock of $100,000? Second, what is the reason for the discounts? Are they the result of operational issues such as late shipments, shipments to wrong locations, etc.? The CRM system would be a good place to start this study. Records of client meetings and contacts might provide a reason for these leakages in profitability. Hopefully, the information contained here will assist in diagnosing and correcting the problem as well as providing a roadmap for future sales to the customer.

Practice Exercise

1. Calculate the profitability of Customer C, based on the following information:

Sales to Customer C:	$5,000,000
Gross Profit percentage	50%
Commission rate	5%
Sales discount rate	5%
Traced overhead cost	10%
Income tax rate	25%

Solutions to the above questions can be downloaded from the **Online Resources** *section of this book on* **www.vibrantpublishers.com**

Chapter Summary

◆ Customers are the lifeblood of a company. Servicing customers and finding new customers should be a top priority of any business.

◆ The goal of any customer relationship is to grow the relationship and make it more profitable.

◆ Customer profitability analysis is becoming increasingly more important in order for a company to be competitive.

◆ Cost accounting provides the information necessary to calculate gross profit on sales. However, this is only half of the profitability analysis. Selling, general and administrative expenses will also heavily impact profitability. A customer profitability system will account for these expenses.

◆ Costs should be traced as much as possible through activity-based costing rather than being allocated to customers and to products. Allocated expenses are often not relevant in the decision-making process.

◆ Relevant and timely information is crucial in successful customer management. A customer resource module (CRM) is a necessary part of the information system in the current business environment. It also can be the starting point for a customer profitability system.

◆ Should the business relationship with unprofitable customers be terminated? This drastic step should be the last resort only after corrective actions have been diagnosed and attempted. Management will also need to consider such things as the future growth in sales, sales mix, etc.

Glossary

Absorbed overhead – the amount of overhead costs that have been absorbed by the products and services sold by a company

Actual overhead – the amount of overhead costs that have actually been incurred by a company

Allowed overhead – the amount of overhead costs that need to be included in the products and services of a company under flexible budgeting

Balance sheet – a financial statement that gives a snapshot of a company's resources (assets), obligations (liabilities), and owners' equity

Beginning inventory – the stock of raw materials, in-process materials, and finished products held by a company at the start of the period (year/quarter)

Breakeven point (BEP) – the point at which a company's total revenues are equal to the total costs

Broad Averaging – a type of costing system that allocates Indirect costs to products/services/departments by averaging

Contribution income statement – a statement of a company's income that shows variable costs and fixed costs separately

Contribution margin – equals (Revenues – Variable costs)

Contribution margin percentage – equals (Contribution margin/ Revenues)

Conversion costs – equals (Direct manufacturing labor costs + Manufacturing overhead costs)

Cost object – a product or a service to which costs need to be traced or allocated

Cost of goods manufactured – cost incurred in manufacturing products over the period (year/quarter)

Cost of goods sold – cost incurred in manufacturing products that were sold during the period (year/quarter), irrespective of when the products were manufactured

CVP analysis – an analysis that shows the relationship between costs, volume, and profit

Direct costs – costs that can be cost-effectively traced to a cost object

Direct cost variance – equals (Actual Direct Costs – Standard (or budgeted) Direct Costs)

Direct manufacturing labor costs – labor costs incurred in manufacturing a product that can be cost-effectively traced to a cost object

Direct material costs – cost of raw materials incurred in manufacturing a product that can be cost-effectively traced to a cost object

Direct method for support department cost allocation – a method of allocating Indirect costs of support departments to operating departments where no allocation is done from one support department to another

Direct variance – the difference between actual and standard (or budgeted) revenue or Direct costs

Dual-rate method for support department cost allocation – a method of allocating Indirect costs of support departments to operating departments by using separate pools for fixed and variable costs

Ending inventory – the stock of raw materials, in-process materials and finished products held by a company at the end of the period (year/quarter)

Fixed budgeting – a method of evaluating Indirect cost variance where the budgeted costs are held fixed, irrespective of the volume of production

Fixed costs – costs that do not change with the volume of production, generally over a relevant range

Flexible budgeting – a method of evaluating Indirect cost variance where the budgeted costs are computed on the basis of the volume of production

Gross profit – equals (Revenues – Cost of goods sold)

Income statement – reports the net income earned by a company over a period (year/quarter)

Indirect costs – costs that cannot be cost-effectively traced to a cost object. These costs are allocated to cost objects

Indirect manufacturing costs – costs of manufacturing that cannot be traced to a cost object

Indirect variance – the difference between actual and standard (or budgeted) Indirect costs

Inventoriable costs – costs that can be shown as an inventory in a company's balance sheet until a sale takes place

Inventory – stock of raw materials, in-process, and finished products held by a company until a sale takes place

Margin of safety – equals (Budgeted revenue – Breakeven revenue)

Net profit – the profit earned by a company after deducting all expenses from the revenues

Operating income – the income of a company before considering interest and income tax payments. Also called EBIT (Earnings Before Interest and Tax).

Operating leverage (Degree of operating leverage) – equals (Contribution margin/Operating income)

Opportunity cost – income forgone by choosing a particular alternative

Period costs – costs that cannot be inventoried and appear in a company's income statement in the period they were incurred

Prime costs – equals (Direct material costs + Direct manufacturing labor costs)

Reciprocal method of support department cost allocation – a method of allocating Indirect costs of support departments to operating departments where support department costs are allocated to each other over and over again before allocating them to operating departments

Revenue – money earned by a company on account of sales and other activities

Revenue variance – the difference between actual and standard (or budgeted) revenue

Semi-variable costs – costs that have a fixed cost component and a variable cost component

Single-rate method – a method of allocating Indirect costs of support departments to operating departments by using a single pool for both fixed and variable costs

Spending variance – equals (Actual overhead – Allowed overhead)

Step-down method – a method of allocating Indirect costs of support departments to operating departments where support department costs are allocated to each other once before allocating them to operating departments

Unit costs – cost of a single unit of the product or service

Variable costs – costs that change with the volume of production in direct proportion

Volume variance – equals (Allowed overhead – Absorbed overhead)

Notes

Made in the USA
Columbia, SC
08 February 2025